Charles Henry Eden

The Home of the Wolverene and Beaver

Or, fur-hunting in the wilds of Canada

Charles Henry Eden

The Home of the Wolverene and Beaver
Or, fur-hunting in the wilds of Canada

ISBN/EAN: 9783337297992

Printed in Europe, USA, Canada, Australia, Japan

Cover: Foto ©Andreas Hilbeck / pixelio.de

More available books at **www.hansebooks.com**

THE HOME

OF THE

WOLVERENE AND BEAVER;

OR,

𝔉ur-hunting in the 𝔚ilds of 𝔔anada.

BY

. CHARLES HENRY EDEN,

Author of "*Australia's Heroes,*" "*The Fortunes of the Fletchers,*"
&c., &c.

—

PUBLISHED UNDER THE DIRECTION OF
THE COMMITTEE OF GENERAL LITERATURE AND EDUCATION,
APPOINTED BY THE SOCIETY FOR PROMOTING
CHRISTIAN KNOWLEDGE.

LONDON:

SOCIETY FOR PROMOTING CHRISTIAN KNOWLEDGE,

NORTHUMBERLAND AVENUE, CHARING CROSS, W.C.:
97, WESTBOURNE GROVE, W.; 43, QUEEN VICTORIA STREET, E.C.
BRIGHTON: 135, NORTH STREET,
NEW YORK: E. & J. B. YOUNG & CO.

PREFACE.

N the following pages I have en
deavoured to give an account
of the various methods employed by Fur-hunters for the
capture of the animals whose
skins form so important an
article of commerce in the
three continents of Europe,
Asia, and America; and whilst
so doing I have given a brief outline of the appearance and habits of the animals themselves, together
with such anecdotes as I thought would prove
interesting to the general reader. As a couple of
hundred pages devoted to trapping alone must of
necessity be somewhat dull, I have attempted to
lighten the volume by some account of the Settlement on the Columbia River founded by Mr. John
Jacob Astor, making use of the two most authentic

records, namely, Washington Irving's "Astoria," and Mr. A. Ross's "Adventures on the Oregon River." For the natural history portion of the book I have also followed the best authorities, namely, Messrs. Audubon and Bachman, Sir John Richardson, and Mr. Samuel Hearne.

My original intention was to change the scene from the Canadian forests to the prairie land of the Far West, with its wandering bands of warlike Indians and larger *Fauna*—the buffalo and the grizzly bear, but the space at my command prevented this, and I have confined myself solely to forest hunting and trapping. Whether the reception accorded to this little volume will justify me in supplementing it with another, remains to be seen.

C. H. EDEN.

HOME OF THE WOLVERENE AND BEAVER;

OR,

Fur-hunting in the Wilds of Canada.

CHAPTER I.

"THE keeper said the ice was dangerous towards the head of the mere; and you know I told Mrs. Marshall I would bring you back in safety, so don't venture too far in that direction, George," cried Paul Gresham to his companion, as both lads, having buckled on their skates, prepared to enjoy a good forenoon's amusement on the fine sheet of frozen water that stood within the boundary of Mr. Marshall's park.

"Never fear, old Paul. You know I am only a feather-weight," laughed George, launching himself upon the smooth surface, which had been swept free of all obstructions by a small boy from the village, closely followed by Rover, a pet retriever, whose anxiety to keep near his master throughout the mazes and twirlings of his course often brought the faithful animal to dire grief.

" The dog is a nuisance," muttered Paul, who, less experienced in the art of skating than his younger companion George Marshall, had nearly fallen headlong over Rover in one of his unexpected turns ; " he'll knock me off my pins in a minute. Can't you keep him on the bank, George," he cried, raising his voice and pointing to the dog.

"All right ; I'll amuse him until you feel your ice-legs under you," replied the latter, and making for the bank he provided himself with a stick, which he threw far away towards the head of the lake for the dog to retrieve. Either the animal was disobedient or instinct warned him that the ice in the part where the stick had stopped was unequal to even his light weight, for he paused, whining, and looked back beseechingly at his master, who, unable to account for such strange conduct, was skating towards him at speed.

" Oh, please come back, George," shouted Paul, on seeing the direction his companion was taking ; " even the dog has got sense enough to know the ice is too thin there." But his warning was either unheard or unheeded ; with lightning speed the reckless lad dashed on—there was a sudden cracking, a crash, a dull plunge, a smothered cry, and Paul Gresham was alone upon the mere !

*   *   *   *   *   *

"Doctor, you must tell me the whole truth. Are they both in danger ? Tell me, I entreat you," said poor Mrs. Marshall, wringing her hands in the deepest grief and agitation.

"Your son, madam, will do well enough. How matters will turn out with young Gresham I am unable yet to say. But I must lose no time now. Be good enough to order more hot water to the lads' room immediately."

"Certainly, doctor, certainly," said the anxious mother, glad of any occupation, however trivial, that tended to the relief of the sufferers ; "but may I not see George ?"

"To be sure you may the moment he awakes, but he is in a sound sleep at present, and must not be disturbed."

When George Marshall opened his eyes some six hours after the preceding short conversation, he found his mother seated by his pillow and anxiously awaiting his earliest movement.

"My darling, are you better now ?"

"Never mind me, mother, I'm all right. How is Paul?"

"Paul is very ill, my dear, and must be kept perfectly quiet."

"Then I must go and see him," and the lad made an effort to rise, but fell back exhausted in the bed. "He has saved my life," he murmured, "and I am unable even to nurse him. You know that it is through me that Paul got under the ice, don't you, mother?" he ran on impetuously, notwithstanding Mrs. Marshall's efforts to restrain him. "I saw him coming towards me, pushing a hurdle before him and shouting to me to keep quiet for a moment, and not break the rotten edge any more by my struggles. In my fright I paid no attention to his advice, and, clutching at the hurdle too suddenly, the ice gave way all round. Paul managed to get the hurdle out of the water again, and had helped me on to it, when his hands became numbed and he sank. Remember, mother, he could have saved himself had he liked, but he had promised you to bring me back safely, and at the peril of his own life he kept his word."

The above sentence will give the reader as good an idea of the catastrophe as a longer description. On seeing his companion immersed, Paul Gresham remembered some hurdles that were stacked near the

edge of the lake, one of which the lads had used for
a seat while putting on their skates. Aided by this
he had managed to extricate his friend, but nearly
at the cost of his own life. Luckily the small boy
who had swept away the snow was lurking about
in the neighbourhood, greedy for coppers or any
remnants of the luncheon that the young people
had brought out with them; and on seeing the
accident, had given the alarm to some labourers
who were working in a field adjoining the park,
and who soon placed George in safety, though the
recovery of Paul was a more tedious process, for
the little stream that fed the lake, and whose current caused the rottenness of the ice, had drifted
him beneath it. Some ten or fifteen minutes
elapsed before the inanimate body was brought to
the surface, and carried on a hurdle to the Hall,
whither George had preceded him, borne in the
same manner. For many hours the struggle between life and death was close, and only by the
vigilance and skill of Doctor Inglis was conscious-
ness at length restored, and it was three good
weeks before Paul Gresham was able to leave his
bed, and as many more before the doctor finally
took leave and pronounced him once more sound in
wind and limb.

And now I must endeavour to enlighten the

reader a little regarding the two lads thus abruptly introduced, with one of whom this story is mainly concerned.

Mr. Robert Gresham, the father of Paul, was a large West Indian proprietor, having inherited sugar plantations and a coffee estate in Demerara from a distant cousin, of whose existence he was almost unaware. His early life had been a fierce struggle with poverty, an actual fight for the bare necessaries of life, under the burthen of which he had seen his young wife pass away, leaving him alone to face the bitter world with a baby only a few weeks old. The winter that witnessed her departure had barely brightened into spring, and the grass was not yet green upon her grave when the intelligence of his cousin's death reached him, and he found himself suddenly lifted from penury to the enjoyment of a large fortune. But though wealth came to the widower, the power to enjoy it was wanting. What would not one hundredth part of the sum, now yearly his, have been to him in the days not long since past ? It would have brought health and bloom to the fair cheek that poverty compelled him to watch growing daily more wan and pale, beneath the pinching fingers of want ; it would have brought peace to the aching heart, and proper nourishment to the feeble frame. It was not to be—Gertrude Gresham faded from this world six weeks after the birth of her son Paul, and in her grave lay buried all the hopes of her sorrowing husband. True, he loved the child, loved him tenderly, and spared no time nor trouble in the guidance of his infancy ; but still there was a void within Robert Gresham's breast, a vacancy that paternal affection alone was insufficient to fill up. " You are young, rich, and of good family, why don't you marry again, Gresham ?" his friends would ask with some impatience, when they saw the little interest he manifested in worldly matters ; but the pained look of the poor widower touched even the least feeling of them, and they were fain to let him pursue his quiet path, playing with his boy, busied with his books, but oftener still, seeking the most solitary corner of his park, and there brooding silently over her he had loved and lost. At last a letter came from his Demerara agent, announcing a yield of surpassing richness, and Mr. Gresham found himself with a large sum of money on his hands that he hardly knew how to dispose of. On the morrow therefore he went to London and looked up his old schoolfellow, Tom Waring, now a shining light on the Stock Exchange.

" Never mind the three per cents," said the broker, " try a venture with it, old fellow. If you don't

pull off trumps it won't so much matter, for the loss
will not affect you, and you *may* double your stake.
Besides it will be some amusement for you, and
drag you out of your den in Surrey. What do you
say? Shall I plunge for you?"

It was in all good-feeling and with the very best
intentions that honest Tom thus spoke, little
thinking that he had raised a passion of whose
existence its owner himself was totally ignorant.
Robert Gresham found in the various chances of
the money market an excitement which weaned
him from his sorrow, and ere long engrossed his
whole being. Under its influence he became
another person. All lethargy was thrown aside,
and he seemed to have stepped into his natural
career, that of a bold and successful speculator.
His luck or his skill were enormous, and he soon
amassed great wealth, while his financial ability and
integrity became of European reputation.

Paul's early days were too uneventful to need
narrating. At twelve years of age he went to
Eton, and there met George Marshall, who had
been commended to him by his father, by whom
Mr. Marshall was held in great esteem both as a
private friend and also as one of the most enterprising partners in the Hudson's Bay Company.
Though the two lads had often heard of each other,

accident had hitherto prevented their meeting, for
the country seats of their respective fathers were
situated widely apart, but once thrown together
similarity of tastes soon firmly united them, acquaintance grew into intimacy, and intimacy ripened
into a strong and durable friendship. It was during
a visit to Mr. Marshall's place in Lancashire, in
the Christmas holidays of 1851, that the ice adventure with which this chapter is opened took place.
Paul Gresham was then a lad of fifteen, tall, slight,
blue-eyed, but dark haired; a pretty boy enough,
and likely, the women said, to grow into a remarkably handsome man. In disposition he was frank
and generous, though perhaps a trifle exacting
amongst his inferiors, the result of having had his
own way too much when a child. Three years at
Eton, however, had done wonders for him, and I
think I may safely say that Paul Gresham was
generally beloved.

George Marshall was one year Paul's junior, and
looked up to the latter with a veneration that we
may seek in vain amongst any but schoolboys.
All lads seem to delight in setting up an idol, and
the hero thus exalted can (according to them) do
no wrong. That the object of this worship ever
did anything whatever to merit such devotion, I am
unable to ascertain, but have incontestable proof

that he led his youthful followers into numberless scrapes, follies, and extravagances, all, however, of a venial nature, and quite unworthy of record.

At the close of the Christmas holidays George had to return to Eton alone, Paul being ordered to the seaside to recruit his health. Easter, however, again saw the lads together, and they thus continued until the close of 1854, when Paul went to Oxford, to be followed the succeeding spring by his chum George. How they alternately read, idled, and were once both rusticated, I need not relate, for it has little bearing upon this story. Their parents were rich, and each of the young men had an ample allowance, so good indeed as to prevent their incurring college debts, a fact for which one of them had cause shortly afterwards to be deeply thankful, for it is quite hard enough to encounter the world single-handed without being handicapped with a mill-stone of college liabilities round your neck at the very start.

Time rolled on until 1857. It was a glorious spring morning and the sun shone merrily down on the smooth grass plots and sparkling fountain of —— College. Bursts of laughter and half snatches of song came through the open windows of one of the best sets of rooms in Oxford, and the unfortunate reading man, working hard for a fellow-

ship in the room below, groaned inwardly as he
stuffed his thumbs in his ears, and bent his head
yet lower over Aristophanes, in the vain hope of
shutting out the mirthful sounds, as he murmured,
" Gresham having another breakfast. The noise at
his wine last night kept me awake until past mid-
night: What a mercy it will be when he leaves ;
and yet he 's a good fellow too."

Had the reading man known how shortly his
wish would be accomplished, he had perhaps been
less willing to frame it.

" Surely I hear some one at the oak. Open
the door, George, and let us see who it is."

George Marshall arose, did as his host desired,
and a boy entered the room with an envelope in
his hand, saying, " A telegraphic message for Mr.
Gresham."

A blank fell upon the faces of the ten or dozen
young men seated round the well-furnished breakfast table, at these ominous words ; for at that date
a telegraphic communication *was* ominous ; the
wires were not then used for the every-day purposes
of the world at large, and only on occasions of importance, such as accident, illness, or death, was
the " lightning message" employed. Small wonder,
then, that the hearts of the guests sank within them,
and notwithstanding the well-bred remonstrances

of Paul, the merry meeting was broken up, and the young man found himself alone with George Marshall.

"Don't move, old fellow," he said, as the latter showed signs of departing. "Wait until I see what it can be."

He held the envelope still unopened in his hand, a deadly pallor on his face, and a huskiness in his voice betraying the emotion he vainly strove to repress. With an effort he tore the cover off, glanced his eye over the unwelcome missive, and whilst holding it out towards George, dropped senseless in his chair.

Robert Gresham was dead—had died suddenly, so people said, after the arrival of the American mail which announced the failure of one of the largest houses in New York. A *post mortem* examination showed that the heart was the actual cause of death, but its action must have been arrested by some sudden mental shock, otherwise, pronounced the faculty, he might have lived for years. Many were the surmises in the financial world as to the amount of the dead man's fortune, and great was the surprise when it became known that he had left nothing, that all his property both in England and in the West Indies was heavily mortgaged, and that little would revert to his only son except the few thousands arising from the sale of the furniture. Singularly fortunate at first, success had rendered him incautious, and latterly losses had fallen upon him thickly and heavily. Still he would have pulled through had it not been for the unforeseen failure of the great American house, but this completely ruined him, and it was the paragraph in the newspapers recording this event that caused his death.

Paul bore the reverse nobly. To say that he did not feel the alteration in his fortune would be untrue; no young man brought up with unlimited money can see himself reduced to penury without regret; but it can be safely affirmed that the loss of his father by far outweighed the loss of his fortune. He at once threw up his rooms at ——, and at Mr. Marshall's request went down to the quiet hall, where, six years before, he had so narrowly escaped drowning.

Mr. Marshall was Robert Gresham's only executor, and much that worthy man pondered on what would be the best career for Paul, whom he loved as though he were his son. The young man, however, relieved him of all anxiety on this score, by saying, "You are one of the directors of the Hudson's Bay Company, cannot you send me out there as a clerk or something?"

"Good gracious, Paul, you would be frozen!" cried kind-hearted Mrs. Marshall; but the young man was unwavering, and in talking it over with his wife, Mr. Marshall said—

" He might do many a worse thing, my dear. The pay will be small enough at first, but if he had the wealth of Golconda he couldn't spend it in Rupert's Land. He will learn a good business practically, and I will see to his advancement. I also hope that we shall save enough from the wreck of the property to clear the West Indian estates, but to accomplish this I must have every penny. Altogether, the boy has shown a great deal of good sense, and in nothing more than in this his last determination."

Three months after the receipt of the telegraphic message—the word " telegram " was unknown then —Paul Gresham took leave of George Marshall on the deck of the Cunard steam ship *Baltic*, bound for Halifax, and I shall endeavour to pourtray his life in the wild western land, the home of the moose, the wolverene, and the beaver.

CHAPTER II.

A FINE passage of nine days brought the *Baltic* in safety to Halifax, the capital of the colony of Nova Scotia. The appearance of the city is very striking, from its being built on a slope, which rises gradually more than two hundred feet above the sea, the lower portion being occupied by warehouses and wharves crowded with shipping, above which are seen the public buildings and fine dwelling-houses intermingled, while the summit of the rise is crowned by a massive granite citadel, and an edifice in whose lofty tower is fixed the town clock, which is thus rendered visible from all parts of the town. The streets are laid out at right angles, and are spacious and handsome, though there is little uniformity in the appearance of the houses, some of them being built of stone or brick, others, equally attractive, of wood neatly painted, while many are stuccoed or plastered. But perhaps the most prominent features of Halifax are its beautiful harbour and dockyard. The

former is one of the finest in the world, extending
nearly sixteen miles inland, and accessible at all
times to ships, however great may be their draught
of water. Opposite the town, where vessels usually
anchor, its breadth is about a mile, and on its
smooth surface is generally seen the graceful hull of
one or more British men-of-war, forming portion of
the North American and West Indian fleet, who
repair to this charming place both to refit and to
enable the crews to shake off the sickness too often
engendered by a lengthened cruise amongst the
fever-stricken islands of the tropics. Beyond the
town the harbour contracts to a quarter of a mile
in width, and finally expands into a noble sheet of
water comprising an area of about ten square
miles, called Bedford Basin. A small arm branching
off from the harbour a short distance below the city
extends inland to within half a mile of this basin,
forming the peninsula on which the city is built.
The dockyard covers an area of fourteen acres, and
is one of the finest in the world out of England.

Paul made but a short stay in this pleasant
place, and when he took his passage in a steamer
bound to Montreal, he carried away with him a
vivid recollection of the bright eyes of some of the
young ladies, for no city in the world can produce
prettier faces than the capital of Nova Scotia.

The voyage up the mighty St. Lawrence, and past the city of Quebec I shall not attempt to describe, suffice it to say that Paul arrived at Montreal in due course, and was warmly welcomed by Mr. Tanner, the agent of the Hudson's Bay Company, to whom he brought letters of introduction from Mr. Marshall.

Montreal is worthy of a few descriptive words, being the largest city in British North America. It is situated at the south side of a large island thirty miles in length by ten in breadth at its widest parts, at the confluence of the St. Lawrence and Ottawa rivers. The city consists of an upper and a lower town, the former of which has wide streets and handsome buildings, while the latter presents a cramped and gloomy appearance, owing to its narrow streets and the French fashion which there prevails of closing the windows with dark iron shutters. Being at the head of the ship navigation Montreal displays great commercial activity. At the time of which we are now speaking, 1857, it was the head-quarters of the troops in North America, and also the see of an Anglican Bishop, who is the Metropolitan of Canada, whilst its population numbered nearly 80,000 people.

But I must now leave Paul Gresham to purchase his outfit under the direction of Mr. Tanner, whilst I

lay before the reader a sketch of the North American fur trade, with which is embodied the history
of the Hudson's Bay Company. Concerning
the latter opulent body but little is known
to the world at large, for it has never been their
policy to court publicity. Such fragments as have
from time to time appeared are fraught with interest,
and if I am somewhat minute in my description, it
is because the subject has been but little handled,
and is of a nature to repay the reader.

In the year 1670, King Charles II. granted a
charter to Prince Rupert, Christopher Duke of
Albemarle, William Earl of Craven, Henry Lord
Arlington, Anthony Lord Ashley, Sir John
Robinson, Sir Robert Viner, Sir John Griffith, Sir
Philip Carteret, James Hayse, John Kirke, Francis
Millington, William Prettyman, John Fenn, and
John Portman and their successors. Its purpose
was to encourage the associates to search for the
north-west passage, and to establish a trade in furs,
minerals, and "other considerable commodities."
It conveyed to the Company a grant of "the sole
trade and commerce of all those seas, straits, bays,
rivers, lakes, creeks and sounds, in whatever latitude
they shall be, that lie within the entrance of the
straits commonly called Hudson's Straits, together
with all the lands and territories upon the countries,

coasts, and confines of the sea, bays, lakes, rivers, creeks and sounds aforesaid," that were not previously granted to or in the possession of any British subjects, or those of any other Christian prince. All mines of gold, silver, gems or precious stones, discovered, or to be discovered, within those territories and limits, were also conveyed to the Company. Of the territory itself, they were constituted free and absolute proprietors, on condition of paying yearly the sovereign two elks and two black beavers ; but this only whenever the sovereign should be within the limits of their territory. The Company had power to make laws, constitutions and ordinances, and to provide pains, penalties, and punishments for their violation ; whilst fines for the breach of laws thus made, were to go to the Company. There was, however, one limitation to these powers ; the laws, constitutions, orders, and ordinances which the Company might make, and the fines and amercements which they might impose, were required to be "reasonable, and not contrary or repugnant, but as near as may be agreeable to the law, statutes or customs of the realm."

How complete was the monopoly intended to be conveyed by Charles II. may be seen by the stipulation on the part of the King, that no other subjects of Great Britain, except the few favoured individuals forming the Company, should even visit the territories granted, contrary to the true meaning of the charter, that is to say, for trading purposes—all other subjects of the crown were expressly forbidden to visit or trade at any of these places, unless specially licensed by the Company, on pain of incurring the royal displeasure, and the forfeiture of goods. Offenders might be bound in the penalty of a thousand pounds not again to trade within this exclusive domain. The Company had full power to equip armed vessels, and send them with men and ammunition to any of their forts, factories, or places of trade, appointing commanders and officers by commission under the common seal. They had the right of making war or concluding peace with any non-Christian prince or people within the territories covered by their charter. They might build castles, forts, or fortifications and garrison them, and lay out towns and villages; whilst any persons, not members of the Company, whether British subjects or not, who should sail into Hudson's Bay, or enter their territory without leave, were liable to be seized and sent to England—in short the power of the new Company was practically unlimited, and the monopoly as complete as the inclination of the monarch, and ink, parchment and lawyers could make it.

For many years, for nearly a century indeed, the Hudson's Bay Company confined their operations to the coast. The fur-bearing animals were in great abundance, the Indian tribes in the vicinity captured them, brought the skins into the nearest fort or factory, and exchanged them for powder, rifles, rum, or some other European commodity. Thus far the Company had had it all their own way; no adventurous traders entered their sacred bay, and a more close and lucrative trade was developed than their most sanguine dreams had ever led them to expect. But a rival was already afield, and attacking their preserves; an enemy not arriving by sea—that they could easily have stopped—but working up from the interior of Canada, the direction in which they were most defenceless.

From the earliest settlement of Canada by the French the fur trade was recognised as of the first importance to the colony, and to procure a supply of skins the Indians were encouraged to penetrate into the country, being generally accompanied by some of the Canadians, who found means to induce the more distant tribes to bring their peltry to the settlements for sale or barter. These adventurous men fell so much in love with the wild life that they led amongst the Indians, that they only returned to civilisation at long intervals, and

gradually became a distinct class known as
coureurs des bois or wood-rangers. Without their
aid the merchant would have been unable to com-
municate with the distant tribes, and the fur trade
would have fallen to the ground, for it is needless
to say that all valuable animals in the vicinity of
the settlements had been long since destroyed.
Therefore acknowledging their value as "go-
betweens," the traders each employed a certain
number of *coureurs*, whom they equipped on credit,
and despatched into the interior. Three or four of
these men would unite their stock, place all their
property in a birch-bark canoe, which they worked
themselves, and would then paddle up the almost
unknown rivers with which Canada abounded, until
they reached a tribe whose hunting-ground seemed
rich enough to repay them. There the light-
hearted Frenchmen would throw aside the garb of
civilisation, would don the attire and lead the life of
the savage, having each taken to himself an Indian
wife. At the expiration of a year or eighteen
months they would return to the settlements, the
frail canoe almost sinking under its load of costly
furs. During their stay in town, their life was one
scene of reckless extravagance and wild dissipation,
insomuch that in fifteen days they often squandered
the hardly-earned gains of as many months. Of

course the merchants took no steps to check such license, for the sooner poor Baptiste had spent his money, the sooner he would be ready to start afresh into the wilderness.

But there were a class of men in Canada to whom the licentious manners of the *coureurs des bois* gave great offence ; these were the Roman Catholic missionaries, who laboured unceasingly to convert the natives, and beheld their efforts brought to nought and their teachings held up to ridicule by men who professed themselves to be members of the Christian faith. They accordingly exerted their influence for the suppression of the *coureurs*, and so far succeeded that no one was allowed to go up country and traffic with the Indians without a license from the Government.

At first these permits were only granted to men of good character, but gradually they came to be bestowed as rewards on officers and their widows, who, if unwilling to use them themselves, were allowed to sell them to the merchants, who in turn supplied them to the *coureurs des bois*, whom they employed as agents; thus the evil again sprang up in greater force than ever, and not until military posts were established at the confluence of the large lakes, was the license of the wood-rangers checked, and trade protected from the consequences resulting from their improper conduct. A good class of respectable people, chiefly retired officers, also prosecuted the trade in person, and gave it a better tone. Sir Alexander Mackenzie, to whose works I am indebted for much of the information here conveyed, says, " These persons and the missionaries having combined their views at the same time, secured the respect of the natives and the obedience of the people necessarily employed in the laborious parts of this undertaking. These gentlemen denominated themselves commanders, and not traders, though they were entitled to both those characters ; and, as for the missionaries, if sufferings and hardships in the prosecution of the great work which they had undertaken deserved applause and admiration, they had an undoubted claim to be admired and applauded : they spared no labour and avoided no danger in the execution of their important office, and it is to be seriously lamented that their pious endeavours did not meet with the success which they deserved ; for there is hardly a trace to be found beyond the cultivated parts of their meritorious functions."

In the year 1763 Canada passed from the French to the British, and for a short time the fur trade languished, for the interior of the country was but little known to the new rulers, and the *coureurs des bois* were naturally shy of serving masters they had always been taught to regard as enemies. In the year 1766, however, it revived, and the competition between rival private traders grew fierce and was productive of the worst results. The trade from its very nature was carried on in the wilderness, far away from legal restraint, and where underhand methods of gaining an advantage over a competitor could be employed unchecked. Mackenzie says, " The consequence was not only the loss of commercial benefit to the persons engaged in it, but of the good opinion of the natives, and the respect of these men, who were inclined to follow their example ; so that with drinking, carousing, and quarrelling with the Indians along their route and among themselves they seldom reached their winter quarters, and if they did it was generally by dragging their property upon sledges, as the navigation was closed up by the frost. When at length they were arrived the object of each was to injure his rival trader in the opinion of the natives as much as was in their power by misrepresentation and presents, for which the agents employed were peculiarly calculated. They considered the command of their employer as binding on them, and however wrong or irregular the transaction, the responsibility rested upon the principal who directed

them. This is Indian law. Thus did they waste
their credit and their property with the natives, till
the first was past redemption and the last was
nearly exhausted, so that towards the spring in
each year the rival parties found it absolutely
necessary to join and make one common stock of
what remained for the purpose of trading with the
natives, who could entertain no respect for persons
who had conducted themselves with so much irregu-
larity and deceit. The winter, therefore, was one
continual scene of disagreements and quarrels. If
any one had the precaution or good sense to
keep clear of these proceedings he derived a pro-
portionable advantage from his good conduct, and
frequently proved a peace-maker between the
parties. To such a height had they carried this
licentious conduct that they were in a continual
state of alarm, and were even frequently stopped
to pay tribute on their route into the country;
though they had adopted the plan of travelling
together in parties of thirty or forty canoes, and
keeping their men armed, which sometimes, indeed,
proved necessary for their defence."

In the face of these evils, the good results that
must accrue from uniting their parties became
apparent to all, and during the winter of 1783-4
the merchants of Canada, engaged in the fur trade,

formed a junction of interests, under the name of the North-West Company; and being joined in 1787 by a rival company, the new association had no competitor except the Hudson's Bay Company, and soon grew into a gigantic and wealthy concern, whose branches spread throughout the country, and whose posts were found on the furthest frontier.

The method by which the North-West Company was established and worked is so peculiar that a few words regarding it can hardly be out of place. It may be said to have been supported entirely upon credit, for, whether the capital belonged to the proprietor or was borrowed it equally bore interest, for which the association was annually accountable. It consisted of twenty shares, un-equally divided among the persons concerned, and of these, a certain proportion was held by the people who managed the business in Canada, who were styled agents. It was the duty of the latter to import the necessary goods from England, store them at their own expense at Montreal, pack and forward them to the starting-place of the canoes, and supply whatever cash might be wanting for outfits, &c. ; as compensation for this extra trouble the agents received, in addition to the profit on their shares, a commission on the amount of the

accounts, which they made out annually, keeping
the venture of each year distinct. Two of them
went annually to the Grande Portage at the mouth
of the Winnipeg River, on the north-west shore of
Lake Superior, to manage and transact the business there and at the intermediate stations, besides
collecting, packing, and forwarding to England all
the Company's furs, on which they received a small
commission. Altogether the position of an agent
in the North-West Company was a highly desirable
one in a worldly point of view, for they amassed
enormous wealth, and were regarded as American
nabobs.

The remaining shares were held by the proprietors, who were obliged to winter in the wilds,
and manage the business part of the concern with
the Indians, aided by their respective clerks, &c.
They were not supposed to furnish either capital
or credit, and if they gained any capital by the
business, it remained in the hands of the agents at
a fixed rate of interest. Some of them, from their
long service and influence, held double shares, and
were allowed to retire whenever they thought fit,
retaining one share and making over the other to a
younger man who succeeded to the more onerous
part of the business, and in this manner the clerks
and subordinate officers of the Company were

provided for and stimulated to perform their duty with zeal and alacrity, for their own interests were identical with those of their employers.

In the year 1788 the total amount of the Company's capital was only forty thousand pounds, but by the exertion, enterprise, and industry of the proprietors, it more than tripled itself in eleven years, and as an investment surpassed anything known in America. Washington Irving says, " Sometimes one or two partners, recently from the interior posts, would make their appearance in New York, in the course of a tour of pleasure and curiosity. On these occasions there was always a degree of magnificence of the purse about them, and a peculiar propensity to expenditure at the goldsmiths and jewellers, for rings, chains, brooches, necklaces, jewelled watches, and other rich trinkets, partly for their own wear, partly for presents to their female acquaintances ; a gorgeous prodigality, such as was often to be noticed in former times in southern planters and West Indian creoles, when flush with the profits of their plantations."

And now having briefly sketched the constitution of the North-West Company I pass on to the manner in which it was worked.

The agents had to exercise great forethought in ordering goods from England, for the communication was very slow, so slow as to seem now-a-days almost incredible. It was eighteen months from the time that an order left Canada for London before the articles demanded could be forwarded up country from Montreal! And the seeming delay occurred thus. An order was sent to London in October, and the goods could not, owing to the ice, arrive at Montreal before the following summer. In the winter they were sorted and packed into parcels of ninety pounds weight each, and the ice again prevented their further progress until the ensuing spring. Even a longer period was necessary to dispose of the furs obtained in exchange for these goods in the London market ; so that a merchant, allowing that he had twelve months' credit, did not receive any return for the goods, and the necessary expenses attending them, until two years after they were considered as cash, and that they were enabled to afford this and make an enormous profit to boot, shows what a thriving concern the fur trade had become.

The articles necessary for the trade were coarse woollen cloths of different kinds ; blankets ; arms and ammunition ; twist and carrot tobacco ; Manchester goods ; linen and coarse sheetings ; thread, lines, and twine ; common hardware ; cutlery and ironmongery of several descriptions ; brass and

copper kettles and sheet iron ; silk and cotton
handkerchiefs ; hats, shoes, stockings, &c., &c.
Spirituous liquors and provisions were purchased
in Canada, but all the foregoing articles were forwarded from England, and from that day to this no
alteration has taken place in the description of goods
required in the fur trade, and the above list would
apply as well to 1876 as to 1788, for which reason
I have here inserted it.

In describing the Company's mode of working, I
cannot do better than make the following extract
from Sir Alexander Mackenzie, whose book, published in the first year of the present century, has
become rare and is little known, though few records
of travel will better repay the reader. He says :—
"We shall now proceed to consider the number of
men employed in the concern, viz., fifty clerks,
seventy-one interpreters and clerks, one thousand
one hundred and twenty canoe men, and thirty-five
guides. Of these, five clerks, eighteen guides, and
three hundred and fifty canoe men, were employed
for the summer season in going from Montreal to
the Grande Portage, in canoes, part of whom proceeded from thence to Rainy Lake, as will be here-
after explained, and are called Pork-eaters or Goers
and Comers. These were hired in Canada or Montreal, and were absent from the 1st of May to the
C 2

latter end of September. For this trip the guides had from eight hundred to a thousand livres,* and a suitable equipment ; the foreman and steersman from four to six hundred livres ; the middlemen from two hundred and fifty to three hundred and fifty livres, with an equipment of one blanket, one shirt, and one pair of trousers ; and were maintained during that period at the expense of their employers. Independent of their wages, they were allowed to traffic, and many of them earned to the amount of their wages. About one-third of these went to winter, and had more than double the above wages and equipment. All the others were hired by the year, and sometimes for three years ; and of the clerks many were apprentices, who were generally engaged for five or seven years, for which they had only one hundred pounds, provision, and clothing. Such of them as could not be provided for as partners at the expiration of this time were allowed from one hundred pounds to three hundred pounds per annum, with all necessaries, till provision was made for them. Those who acted in the twofold capacity of clerk and interpreter, or were so deno-minated, had no other expectation than the pay-ment of wages to the amount of from one thousand.

* Thirty-two to forty pounds sterling. The value of one hundred livres is four pounds.

to four thousand livres per annum, with clothing and provisions. The guides, who are a very useful set of men, acted also in the additional capacity of interpreters, and had a stated quantity of goods, considered as sufficient for their wants, their wages being from one to three thousand livres. The canoe men are of two descriptions, foremen and steersmen, and middlemen. The two first are allowed annually one thousand two hundred, and the latter four hundred livres each. The first class had what is called an equipment, consisting of two blankets, two shirts, two pair of trousers, two handkerchiefs, fourteen pounds of carrot tobacco, and some trifling articles. The latter had ten pounds of tobacco and all the other articles: those are called North-men or Winterers; and to the last class of people were attached upwards of seven hundred Indian women and children, victualled at the expense of the Company."

As soon as the rivers and lakes were free from ice, which was usually by the beginning of May, the Company's wharf at Montreal presented a busy scene. Numbers of birch bark canoes lay ready to receive their freight, consisting of sixty-five packages (ninety pounds each), an abundant supply of provisions for the eight or ten men constituting the crew of each vessel, and material to repair her

should she rend her frail sides in shooting a rapid.
On first seeing these canoes piled up with goods,
and their gunwales within a few inches of the
water even before the crew had taken their seats, a
stranger would undoubtedly prophesy the disappear-
ance of the vessel and her contents before many
miles were accomplished, but such is the skill of the
Canadian *voyageurs* that accidents rarely happen.
The little fleet paddle from the wharf, shoot the
rapid at St. Anne's—familiar to us in Moore's boat
song—and then consider their journey fairly commenced, for at that spot stands the last church on
the island, dedicated to the reputed tutelary saint
of voyagers.

To follow them minutely in their long passage
to the Grande Portage would be tedious.   The few
scattered homesteads on the river banks are soon
left behind, and they are in the lonely wilderness,
whose echoes are awakened by the song and
mirthful jests of the light-hearted Frenchmen.
Falls are frequently encountered, and rapids that it
would be too dangerous to shoot, and then comes
the labour of a *portage* or a *décharge*, the former
term meaning the transport of both goods and
canoe overland, the latter of the goods alone.
Each man carries two packages on his back
suspended in a sling that passes over the forehead,

and some stout fellows will walk away over rocky, steep ground with three—while four others lift their light craft out of the water, shoulder her, and convey her carefully beyond the obstacle. In a *décharge* the canoe is commonly towed by a strong cord, one man remaining in her to manage and steer. Formerly several of these toilsome operations had to be performed in a day, now there is a canal with smooth water all the way, but alas! the graceful canoe is no longer to be seen paddling on its surface with its motley crew of Canadians and half-breeds; the steam engine has destroyed the romance of the lakes.

At length they arrive in safety within sight of the fort at the Grande Portage, with its large barricade of cedar wood, within which are enclosed the residences for the accommodation of the proprietors and clerks during their short stay there. The North-men and the Pork-eaters shift for themselves as best they can, the former in tents, the latter under their canoes. Hardy and accustomed to face any weather with indifference, the smallest shelter suffices for their simple wants. And now comes the selection of extra men to stay during the winter, the payment of all accounts, the transport of the goods across the nine miles which has gained the Grande Portage its name, and lastly, a few days of eating and drinking and jollification. Mackenzie says, " It is, indeed, very creditable to them as servants, that though they are sometimes assembled to the number of twelve hundred men, indulging themselves in the free use of liquor, and quarrelling with each other, they always show the greatest respect to their employers, who are comparatively but few in number, and beyond the aid of any legal power to enforce due obedience—in short, a degree of subordination can only be maintained by the good opinion these men entertain of their employers which has been uniformly the case since the trade has been formed and conducted on a regular system."

Let us take a peep at the Grande Portage at six o'clock on a July evening, and thus gain some insight into the mode of living current at that remote place. The men have returned from transporting goods over the nine miles that must be traversed to reach unbroken water; some of them have carried two packages of ninety pounds each across, and returned with the same weight of skins, performing the double journey over very rough ground in little more than six hours. They are now dispersed in every direction, some reclining and smoking while their squaws mix their hominee; others, whose domestic arrangements are not so complete, performing this office for themselves, but all, without exception, gesticulating and speaking with a volubility that defies description in a jargon of mixed French, English, and Indian, that is nearly deafening and utterly incomprehensible.

One word here, regarding "hominee," for it is the sole diet given by the Company to their canoe men, and ought to be good stuff to keep up the strength of these hardworking people. Hominee is nothing more than Indian corn and melted fat. The former is prepared before shipment, by boiling it in a strong alkali, which takes off the outer husk; after being well washed and carefully dried, it is fit for use. Corn is the cheapest provision that the Company can procure, but from the expense of transport it cannot be landed at the Grande Portage under twenty shillings the bushel, and a man's daily allowance is a little less than one twentieth part of this, or about ten pennyworth. To prepare it for use, a quart of corn should be boiled for two hours over a moderate fire, in a gallon of water; to which, after it has been on a little while, should be added two ounces of melted suet, which causes the corn to split, and in the time mentioned above makes a pretty thick pudding. Salt must be added after, not during the boiling process, with which it would sadly interfere, and the hominee is

then ready for eating, and is a wholesome, palatable
food, pleasant to the taste, and easy of digestion.
The above quantity is fully sufficient for a man's
subsistence during twenty-four hours, and, as I said
before, with the exception of any fish they may
catch or game they may shoot, is all the Company's
canoe men ever get.

But to return to the fort. If, leaving the
picturesque groups of *voyageurs* and their Indian
belongings, we stroll into the large wooden building that stands nearly in the centre of the enclosure
we shall witness a curious and pleasing sight. At
some half a dozen long rough tables are seated at
least a hundred men, a few of them in the garb of
civilisation, but by far the greater number in a
nondescript dress, half European half Indian, but
in which buckskin is the main constituent. At the
head of the two principal tables, situated at the
opposite end of the hall to the door by which we
entered, are seated two gentlemen, one rather bald,
the other with a palpable wig, and both when they
speak betraying that the land of their birth lay
north of the Tweed. These are the agents from
Montreal, and the reason of one of them wearing a
wig, not an uncommon article in the civilised world
in 1788, but rather out of place on the shores of
Lake Superior—is that he lost his scalp when a

young man ; woke from a peaceful slumber beside
his watch-fire on the Saskatchewan to find the
Blackfeet warriors bending over him, and the keen
knife of the chief about to encircle his temples.
The bitter frost prevented much bleeding, and
Andrew McClosky, after a fearful journey, reached
the settlements, and ultimately completely recovered, though his hair is adorning the belt of
the " Eagle's-ribs " or forming a carrotty fringe to
the chief's leggings. The other men in broadcloth
are the clerks, and the remainder of the company
consists of the guides and interpreters, all of whom
mess at one common table. And the board may
boast of plenty if it has not much variety ; there
seems no lack of salt pork, beef, ham, and venison
in the way of meat, or of Indian corn, potatoes, and
peas as a vegetable adjunct, while to wash down
the good cheer there is either tea or spirits, and
every man may take what he likes and as much as
he thinks fit, for restriction is unthought of. The
language of the interpreters and guides is nearly
as perplexing as that of the canoe-men, but that it
is perfectly intelligible to most of the party is
apparent by the bursts of laughter with which
a story is received, told by a French half-breed
in a lingo that would puzzle Max Müller and
the united wisdom of the Philological Society.

But the days of feasting and relaxation are soon over; then the different detachments enter their canoes and push up into the wilderness, each to encounter the severity of the winter in the best manner it can; and there, until the welcome spring removes from the rivers and watercourses the seal set upon them by the ice king, these hardy men remain, hunting and trapping themselves, inciting the Indian tribes in their vicinity to do likewise, and leading a life that, at its best, must be regarded as one of terrible hardship.

After the despatch of the wintering parties the agents return to Montreal, paddled over the lovely reaches of the Ottawa by their faithful French Canadian boatmen, who venerate the Company as an institution, and almost deify McClosky and his colleague as the representatives of a body potent for good or evil in the eyes of these simple fresh-water sailors.

Such is a brief sketch of the Montreal fur-traders; but meanwhile the Hudson's Bay Company were not idle, and instead of waiting, as hitherto, for the Indians to come to their trading places on the shores of the Bay, pushed outposts in every direction towards the interior, and left no stone unturned to crush or oust their daring rival the North-West Company. The United States also naturally longed for a share of the rich spoil, and in 1809 the Pacific Fur Company was started by an enterprising German-American, John Jacob Astor, whose ambitious views were directed to no less an object than the acquirement, by purchase or otherwise, of the whole fur trade of the Continent. Although the latter association was styled a "Company," it was in reality nothing more than the private speculation of Mr. Astor, who supplied the whole of the capital and appointed all the nominal partners. In the very outset the Pacific Fur Company was unlucky, losing a ship with many valuable stores, and pursued by the bitter enmity of the North-West Company, who were little disposed to tolerate a rival. Added to all this war broke out between Great Britain and the United States in 1812, and thus Mr. Astor was cut off from sea communication with his great central depôt, which was situated at the mouth of the Columbia River in Oregon, and somewhat grandiloquently named "Astoria." Foiled on all sides, the great speculator was compelled to come to terms with his rivals, and on the 16th of October, 1813, the North-West Company took over at a valuation the whole of the goods belonging to the *soi-disant* Pacific Fur Company, and changed the name of the depôt from Astoria to Fort George.

But two such neighbours as the Hudson's Bay and the North-West Companies were hardly likely to remain on amicable terms, more particularly as the former regarded their rivals as interlopers on their sacred territory. For years and years the struggle was continued between them, a struggle in which their hot-blooded followers took part, and in which many valuable lives were lost. At last matters became so serious that Government was compelled to interfere, with the result that the rivals became one, under the name of the senior association, the Hudson's Bay Company. This desirable event took place in the year 1821, and from then to the date of my story no attempts were made to overthrow the monopoly of this now doubly powerful association.

I am conscious that much of the foregoing will prove heavy to the majority of my readers, but nevertheless the subject seemed to me of sufficient interest to warrant its insertion.

CHAPTER III.

"WELL, Mr. Gresham," said the Hudson's Bay agent, one morning after Paul had resided under his hospitable roof at Montreal for a fortnight, during which time he had purchased an outfit under his host's direction, "when do you think you will be ready for a start?"

"I think my kit is pretty complete now," replied the young man, "and I am quite at your disposal. Indeed, the sooner I make a beginning the better, and I am longing to enter upon the wild life of which your head *voyageur* Pierre is never tired of singing the charms."

"Then in that case there need be no further delay, and you can start the day after to-morrow. Mr. Marshall wishes you to learn the varied duties of a fur trader thoroughly, and therefore I have decided on sending you first to Osnaburg House, at the head of Lake Joseph, where you will see the method of trading with the Wood Indians; afterwards we can move you to a prairie station. You will find the life at Osnaburg a very lonely one, but not on the whole uninteresting, particularly if you have any taste for natural history. Mr. Groves, the officer in charge, is a quiet, gentlemanly young man, and I make no doubt that you will both get on capitally together. I am sending Pierre with you in charge of some stores for Osnaburg, and he will soon initiate you into the mysteries of wood-craft."

Within a fortnight from the conversation recorded above, Paul Gresham stepped ashore from the steamer at Thunder Bay—the Grande Portage described in the previous chapter—and was warmly welcomed by the agent at the Company's factory, who, seeing the young man's impatience to reach his ultimate destination, hurried forward the preparations for the departure of the four canoes that would be requisite to transport the stores and luggage to Osnaburg House. Six half-breeds composed the crew of each of the little birch-bark craft, and with a salute of a couple of guns from the fort, answered by a ringing cheer from the *voyageurs*, the long paddle up stream commenced, and Paul Gresham was fairly embarked upon his new life.

How beautiful everything seemed to him, the child of civilisation, who had never before seen nature in her virgin grandeur, her waters unfurrowed by the restless steamer, and her pure air unsullied by the smoke of factory chimneys; and every surrounding was in harmony with the wild landscape. The canoe in which he was seated, without a vestige of iron in her composition, loaded within a few inches of the rippling stream; the half-clad boatmen plying their paddles with bare and sinewy arms, chanting the while a wild and plaintive melody to which the water fretting against the rocky ledges, formed a pleasing accompaniment; the ever-changing appearance of the river, now widening out into a little lake embossed with miniature islands, or anon narrowing into a rocky gorge down which the torrent thundered menacingly, requiring strong arms and a steady eye to thread its intricate and foam-covered mazes; the heavy splash as a salmon flung his silver sides aloft into the air; and at intervals a rustling and crackling in the underwood that marked the path of the timid deer flying from the presence of the intruder—man. All was novel, all was beautiful, and Paul felt a load lifted from his breast and replaced by an exhilaration to which he had been a stranger since his father's death. All the past was now to be forgotten, the dream of a life devoted to stormy politics or gentle literature, must now be laid aside for ever; the future lay in his own hands,

and could his lot be cast in a lovelier land? No.
The very river seemed to murmur, "Better abide
by me than breathe the murky and infected air of
the great city," and the graceful hemlock* bowed
her head over the eddy where the curling ripple
loved to fawn at her feet, and whispered, "Yes, live
with me in the wilderness. Am I and my kindred
not sweeter to dwell amongst than crowded
assemblies and gas-tainted theatres?"

But a dull sound, for some time audible, had now
increased to a continuous thunder, and Paul, awaken-
ing from his reverie, asked Pierre the cause. Pierre
Lefranc was a French-Canadian, and a right good
specimen of the breed. From his earliest boyhood
he had led a wild, roving life, first in company with
his father, a *coureur des bois*, latterly by himself,
but ever in the Hudson's Bay service. Brought up
amongst the employés of the Company he regarded
that honourable association as the embodiment of
everything good and powerful in this world. He
lived by the Company, he swore by the Company,
in fact he may almost be said to have lived *for* the
Company. Any one unconnected with them he
regarded with ineffable contempt, and the small
private traders were his abomination. As Mr.
Tanner represented the Company in Canada, Pierre

* Abies Canadensis.

centred all his devotion on him, serving and obeying him with the faithfulness of a spaniel dog, and the unreasoning fidelity of a Highland clansman. Mr. Marshall, the powerful English director, had manifested such unwonted interest in Paul, that the agent resolved on putting him under the guardianship of Lefranc, whose anxiety lest anything should befall his charge was almost laughable to witness. He never took his eyes off him ; if a little spray broke over the gunwale of the canoe, honest Pierre manifested the utmost displeasure and rated the crew so soundly that Paul was obliged to interfere on their behalf; indeed the young man was rather annoyed at being the object of such unwearying solicitude, and longed for the time when he should have learned the manners and customs of the wilds for himself, and be regarded as no longer in need of walking in leading-strings. In appearance Pierre was singularly striking, being of gigantic stature, and having the lower part of his good-natured face concealed by a bushy blonde beard, the admiration of his little wife, a Cree half-breed, who accompanied him everywhere, and was now seated in the canoe with Paul and her herculean husband, who replied to the question addressed to him.

"*Quel est le bruit?* Vat is dat noise? *Mais, Monsieur Paul, c'est la chute*—de fall—de great rapeed, and we must make von liteel portage before ve shall camp pour la nuit—for de night."

Steadily plying their paddles the boatmen speeded the canoes onward, and now a sudden bend in the river brought Paul in full view of the rapid, rushing down a narrow gorge, flanked on either side by pine-clad rocks, whose scarped sides seemed insurmountable to any living thing less active than a chamois.

"Surely we are not going any nearer to that cauldron?" he asked Pierre, pointing towards the seething waters that tore through the defile in a snow-white mass of milky foam. The *voyageur* was too much occupied in guiding the canoe to reply, but his little wife smiled pleasantly, showing her white teeth, and pointing to the rapid, so the young man could only suppose that they actually were about to enter the broken water, and concluded that his best plan was to sit perfectly still and watch how events would turn out.

The canoe containing Paul and Pierre was the leader, and guided by the *voyageur* the heavily laden cockleshell was forced by the sinewy arms of the boatmen against the torrent until even their iron muscles were unable to gain another foot; then with a curve of the steering paddle Lefranc shot towards the rocky wall, and Paul for a moment

closed his eyes, as destruction against its jagged
teeth seemed inevitable; but by another powerful
sweep the danger was averted—within a hair's
breadth though, for by stretching out an arm he
could almost have touched the granite—and guided
solely by the Canadian's paddle the canoe was
borne smoothly forward towards the fall, the noise
of whose roaring waters was almost deafening. By
skilful management the back-water, which is a
portion of every rapid, had been reached, and in a
few seconds the canoe was made fast alongside a
smooth projecting rock that quite sheltered it from
the stream, and the work of unloading commenced
in silence, as far as talking was concerned, for a
six-pounder could hardly have been heard amidst
that mighty unbroken roar, and the human voice
was powerless.

After all the goods had been unladen, the canoe
itself was lifted out of the water by her crew, and
carried carefully over the quarter of a mile of rocky
ground that constituted the portage. Room was
thus made at the little landing-place, when the
next canoe performed the same operation, and
then another, until all four were safely floating
in the smooth reach above the fall. From the
summit of a projecting rock that overhung the
boiling race beneath, Paul watched the movements

of each boat as it approached the rapid, and was then able to form a correct idea of the nerve and skill requisite to overcome the dangers of the situation, and hardly knew which to admire most, the steadiness and obedience of the crew, the good judgment and coolness of the steersman, or the behaviour of the light craft themselves, so frail in their structure that a lady's bodkin would almost pierce their sides, and which yet rode safely where a stronger built and less handy vessel would infallibly have been dashed into a thousand pieces.

After all the goods were re-embarked the flotilla paddled on a couple of miles to escape from the dead roar of the rapid, and then, steering for the shore, the travellers landed and made their camp for the night. This was a far simpler and more speedy operation than the reader would probably imagine. The time was summer, and the climate so mild that none of the extra precautions we are so accustomed to associate with bivouacking in Canada were necessary. The boatmen first knocked up a couple of rough shelters with pine saplings, one for Paul, the other for Pierre Lefranc and his wife, and then betook themselves to fishing for their supper, too hardy to care about even the slight shelter afforded by a few boughs, and quite contented to stretch themselves in their blankets beside

the fires that each party kept burning, not for the
heat that they threw out, but to secure some little
respite from the attacks of insects. During the
summer in Canada, the traveller, particularly if
encamped near marshy ground, finds his leisure
moments fully occupied in warding off the attacks
of poisonous flies and other members of the insect
world. Three different kinds of these tormentors
may be enumerated, viz., the mosquito, the black
fly, and the gnat, who relieve each other in regular
succession, so that their human prey has no respite.
The mosquitoes continue at their posts from dawn
until eight or nine o'clock in the forenoon ; the
black flies then appear, and remain in the field
until sunset ; the mosquitoes again mount guard
until dark, and are finally succeeded by the gnats,
who continue their watch and incessant attacks
until sunrise ; thus each variety has its own hour
and opportunity, their arrangements never clash,
and they are enabled to devote their whole time
and attention to the torture of their unhappy
victims. Paul, who was unseasoned, and whose
succulent beef-fed flesh doubtless held out irresistible attractions to his enemies, suffered greatly,
for the irritation from the bites of these puny insects
is excessive, and the temptation to allay the smart
by scratching intense ; and by incautiously rubbing

the places he would soon have made dangerous
wounds, had not the Violet, Pierre's pretty little
half-breed wife, explained to him the danger of
such a proceeding, and given him some ointment
made from herbs known only to the Indians,
which allayed his pain and prevented any
swelling.

All the Canadian lakes and rivers abound with
fish, and the *voyageur* has scarcely thrown in his
line before a smart tug announces that some
member of the finny tribe has found his bait too
attractive to be withstood. Salmon, trout, fresh-
water herrings, bass, shad, and sturgeon, all are to
be found in plenty, besides a kind called white-
fish, which are annually caught in great numbers by
means of long nets, and on which some of the
Indian tribes almost entirely exist ; indeed several
of the Hudson's Bay Company's outposts are in a
great measure dependent on these fish, dried and
otherwise cured, for their subsistence throughout
the long winters.

To describe the journey from Thunder Bay to
Osnaburg House minutely would be wearisome to
my readers, and perhaps not particularly instruc-
tive, so I shall content myself by saying that on
reaching Rainy Lake the main channel leading to
Winnepeg was quitted, and the little flotilla stood

northward, and entering a much narrower river
arrived eventually at Lake Sal, the furthest that
they could reach by water. Carts were sent down
from Osnaburg House for the stores, and a couple
of horses for Paul and Lefranc, so leaving their
baggage to follow them in the vehicles, the young
man and his companion mounted, and in due
course arrived at their destination.

The Hudson's Bay trading station or fort named
Osnaburg House stands on the north-east end of
Lake Joseph, a considerable sheet of water, abounding with fish, and most beautiful in its scenery.
The station consisted of several dwelling and store
houses, enclosed within a large rectangular barricade
built of stout logs, and having at each of the four
corners a block-house, pierced with loop-holes for
the discharge of musketry and small cannon. The
time was when these safeguards were absolutely
necessary, when the red man hung about the
skirts of the pine forest, watching with the un-
tiring vigilance of his race for some oversight or
carelessness on the part of the white intruders.
Lulled into security by the absolute quiet reigning
around, the little garrison would relax in vigilance,
the gates would sometimes be left open for an
hour at a time, and the cartridges with which the
swivels were loaded became damp and useless.

All this was carefully noted by the keen eye of the unseen foe, and some bright morning, when the rising sun was just shooting its golden rays through the breaks in the gloomy fir, and lighting up the graceful foliage of the maple, the war-whoop would echo from the forest, the Huron was at their gates. Then came the rush for rifle, carbine, and sword, the vain attempt to discharge the neglected ordnance, the shriek of affrighted women, and the deeply uttered curse of men bemoaning their own foolish confidence. What need to follow up the scene further. A dozen pale-face scalps hung in the lodges of the tribe, and the white man was driven forth into the wilderness.

Yes, chief of the Hurons—the War Cloud, the Black Moccassin, the Soaring Eagle, whatever may be your lofty patronymic—you may boast in the council of your triumph over the pale face, and point to the pole on which his locks dangle in the wind, but the white man will return, will return armed with a mightier weapon than rifle and steel, with the fire-water that will kindle your brain at first, but will ultimately rob you of every spark of manhood, and leave you degraded, besotted, lost— so lost that you crouch and fawn to him, your former enemy, nay, that you even submit to be spurned by his foot, for the sake of the poison he will dole out to you to wash away the indignity.

The outworks at Osnaburg House had ceased to be required long before Paul's arrival, and the swivels were honeycombed with age, and hardly fit to fire a blank cartridge as a salute. Their day was past. Civilisation, as the term is understood by the Hudson's Bay Company, had rendered the poor red man mild and inoffensive enough, some of its phases indeed—small-pox for example—had nearly swept him from the face of the earth.

Paul was very warmly received by Mr. Groves, to whom his arrival was an inestimable boon. Any of my readers who have been shut up by an unforeseen accident in a country house, and kept for even a few weeks without any news of the outer world, can faintly imagine what a blessing the arrival of a companion was to the dweller by that lonely lake, one, moreover who had just come out from England, and could tell him of all the great changes that had happened since he himself had quitted the little Somersetshire village in which he nad been brought up. Nor was Pierre Lefranc less welcome, for his skill as a trapper and a hunter was known throughout the Company, and the face of the officer wore quite a cheerful expression as he conducted Paul to the principal house, and pointed out the room allotted to him.

" You have just arrived in time," he said, when Paul, refreshed by a bathe in the lake and a change of clothing, took his seat at the supper table, " for in a few days I expect a party of Ojibbeways in with their furs, and you may depend on their quickening their movements when they find out that a fresh supply of stores have reached the fort."

" And what kind of peltry will they bring ? " asked Paul.

" Oh, principally beaver, and most likely a bear-skin or two. Of course all fur-bearing animals are scarce in this quarter now, but we have a good number of beavers still left, though their skins have sunk enormously in value since the hatters have taken to using silk in place of fur. A beaver skin used to fetch thirty shillings in London, it is now hardly worth a sixth of that sum."

Paul was most anxious to gain every information possible regarding the different animals whose fur renders them so eagerly sought after, and both Mr. Groves and Pierre Lefranc were perfectly willing to satisfy his curiosity, so by questioning them, and keeping his eyes well open he learnt a variety of things regarding the trade, which, as well as I can, I shall endeavour to convey to the reader.

The list of animals whose fur is valuable as
an article of commerce, and whose habitat is within
the Hudson's Bay Territory, is as follows:—beavers;
bears of four kinds, viz., black, brown, white, and
grizzly ; badgers ; buffaloes ; deer, both rein and
red; elks, or moose ; fishers ; foxes of six kinds,
viz., black, silver, cross, red, white, and blue ;
lynxes ; martens ; musquash, or musk rat ; otters ;
seals ; wolves and wolverenes. But the Hudson's
Bay Company, although their principal trade is in
peltry, obtain other valuable articles from the
animals and fishes abounding in the territory. For
example, feathers of all kinds are carefully preserved,
as well as oil from the seal, whale, and sturgeon ;
quills, swans' skins, salted fish and cured salmon,
all help to fill the coffers of the Company; not
forgetting the " castoreum," or, as it is called by the
trappers, " bark-stone," an odoriferous substance
secreted in two glandular sacs near the root of the
beaver's tail. The latter beautiful little animal, so
relentlessly hunted down by man that in many
parts it has entirely disappeared, is so curious in its
habits as to merit a slight description. Doubtless
most of my readers have watched the two captives
at the Zoological Gardens, and smiled at their flat
trowel-like tails. Poor little beasts, they do not
show to advantage as prisoners. To appreciate the

work that can be done with those ugly tails, and
the timber that can be felled by those keen little
teeth, the broad Atlantic must be crossed, and the
animals seen in their native haunts.

The American Beaver (*Castor Fiber*) has long
been regarded with admiration and wonder from
the reports brought in by trappers and others of
its remarkable instinct and sagacity. Audubon,
the great American naturalist, says, "The early
writers on both continents have represented it as a
rational, intelligent and moral being, requiring but
the faculty of speech to raise it almost to an
equality, in some respects, with our own species.
There is in the composition of every man, whatever
may be his pride in his philosophy, a proneness in
a greater or less degree to superstition, or at least
credulity. The world is at best but slow to be
enlightened, and the trammels thrown around us
by the tales of the nursery are not easily shaken off.
Such travellers into the northern parts of Sweden,
Russia, Norway, and Lapland, as Olaus Magnus,
Jean Marius, Leems, &c., whose extravagant and
imaginary notions were recorded by the credulous
Gesner, who wrote marvellous accounts of the
habits of the beavers in Northern Europe, seem to
have worked upon the imaginations and confused
the intellects of the early explorers of our Northern

regions—La Houtan, Charlevoix, Theodut, Ellis, Beltrani, and Cartwright. These last excited the enthusiasm of Buffon, whose romantic stories have so fastened themselves on the mind of childhood, and have been so generally made a part of our education, that we now are almost led to regret that three-fourths of the old accounts of this extraordinary animal are fabulous; and that, with the exception of its very peculiar mode of constructing its domicile, the beaver is, in point of intelligence and cunning, greatly exceeded by the fox, and is but a few grades higher in the scale of sagacity than the common musk-rat."

So says Audubon, a good authority, for he is a native of the same land as the beaver, and devoted much time and labour to ascertain its true habits, but none the less it seems hard to have one's pet belief so ruthlessly demolished.

This animal is a native of both Europe and Asia, but is far more plentiful in North America, from which country we have received the most trustworthy and accurate accounts of its habits. Beavers are gregarious, that is to say, they associate in greater or lesser numbers, and unite their strength for the furtherance of any work necessary to the well-being of the whole amphibious community. But before proceeding further it may be advisable to describe the animal itself, for the sake of those who have never seen it either wild or in captivity.

A full grown male beaver measures a little over two feet from the nose to the root of the tail, and the latter useful member is very broad and flat, tongue-shaped, and covered with angular scales in place of fur.   In shape it resembles a magnified guinea-pig, but only in shape, and I should not degrade the intelligent beaver by comparing it to such a useless little animal did I know any other at all familiar to English readers.   If I were writing in America I should say it resembled the musk-rat, whose acquaintance we shall make further on.   The beaver has an obtuse divided nose, small eyes, and small rounded ears ; its fore-feet are short and slender, with well separated and flexible toes ; with these it conveys food to its mouth, sitting up on its hind quarters, and supported by its flat, leathery-looking tail, much in the same manner as a squirrel.   The hind-feet differ from the fore, and bear a great resemblance to those of a goose, being webbed and having hard, callous soles.   Now we come to the fatal inheritance of the poor beaver, the possession of which causes it to be trapped, shot, hunted down, and generally put to death by its merciless foes—its fur.   This is of two kinds, an upper and an under coat.   The former is of long hair, smooth and glossy, but coarse ; the latter is dense, soft, and silky. In general the fur is of a shining chestnut colour, but it varies considerably, for black beavers are sometimes captured, and white ones are not unknown. At the root of the tail are found the glandular sacs containing the musky unctious substance called castoreum.

Such is the description of the *Castor Fiber*, and now we come to its habits. Before noticing the facts ascertained by modern naturalists, it may not be uninteresting to hear what our forefathers thought of this curious animal, and to notice how intimately fiction and fact are blended together. In Pinkerton's Voyages, vol. I., p. 418, will be found the following :—

"The beaver is met with in some districts of Swedish Lapland, and on the banks of a very large and famous lake, which is said to be twelve miles in circuit. The same lake, as reported, is of an immense and almost unfathomable depth, and in it are many lesser islands. They say the tooth of this animal is reddish, crooked, and almost squared. His tail, by the aid of which he is said to make a house for himself, is broad, rough, and full of scales. The wool, or rather hairs, are sold to the Russians in common, and at a good price ; they purchase also the skin for the covering their under garment with.

E

*   *   *   The force and efficacy of the beaver or castor oil* in various symptoms, is wonderful, too well known to practitioners in medicine to be mentioned by me. It is said to be medicinal for the internal diseases of cattle ; it is said to be of service in frightening and driving away whales, to whom its very smell alone is insufferable; for which reason fishermen, apprehensive of harm from this great fish, are ever provided with the oil of castor. The beaver for this reason is instinctively led to build his house near the banks of lakes and rivers. They saw with their teeth birch trees with which the building is constructed. Whichever of the beavers supplies the place of the sledge, lies upon his back, with his feet upwards, whilst his companions put the wood between his feet as he lies down, and holding it with his teeth, he drags it along to the place destined for building his habitation, together with the wood laid upon it. In this manner one piece of timber is carried after another where they choose. Those who supply the place of the sledge are easily known from the rest by the defect of hair, which is rubbed off by constant action all along the back. At the lake or river where their house is to be

---

* This is, of course, an error of Pinkerton's. The medicinal oil obtained from the Castor-Oil Plant *(Ricinus Communis)* is totally distinct from the substance possessed by the beaver.

built they lay birch stocks or trunks covered with
their bark at the bottom itself, and, forming a
foundation, they complete the rest of the building
with so much art and ingenuity as to excite the
admiration of the beholders. The house itself is of
a round and arched figure, equalling in its circumference the ordinary hut of a Laplander. In this
house the floor is for a bed, covered with branches
of trees, not in the very bottom, but a little above,
near to the edge of the lake or river, so that between
the foundation and the flooring on which the dwelling is supported there is formed, as it were, a cell,
filled with water, in which the stocks of the birch-
tree are put up, on the bark of this the beaver family
who inhabit this mansion feed. If there are more
families under one roof, besides the said flooring,
another resembling the former is built a little above,
which you may not improperly name a second story
in the building. The roof of the dwelling consists
of branches very closely compacted, and projects
out far over the water. You have now, reader, a
house consisting and laid out in a cellar, a flooring,
a hypocaust, a ceiling, and a roof, raised by a brute
animal, altogether destitute of reason and also of the
builders' art, with no less ingenuity than commodi-
ousness. This, too, is an extraordinary instance of
the Divine wisdom and goodness, which, in addition

to the other instinctive actions of brute animals straying through their haunts, should more excite and actuate us to the admiration, praise, and adoration of the Divine Being. In the said cell is an aperture, which serves for a door, through which the beavers go in and out. When they are all abroad, the hunters put a kind of a little fastening on that opening or door in such a manner that, on the entrance of the first beaver, it should fall and close up the whole aperture as far as it goes. Thus shut up, the beaver which is within is hindered from going out, and is taken. But as to what is hitherto related concerning the beaver and his manners I have not attained by my own experience, nor could I learn, because through that whole district where my duty as a missionary lay, this animal never came in my way; but what I have heard from Laplanders inhabiting those places resorted by beavers, I faithfully relate."

So runs old Pinkerton, and there is far more truth than extravagance in what he thus records. The idea of one beaver lying down on its back to be dragged along the ground by its companion is most amusing, and doubtless is the foundation for some of the wondrous anecdotes of rats conveying eggs in a similar manner, that sensational naturalists are fond of recording.

Let us now pass on to modern accounts of the habits of the beaver. It is agreed that they prefer small clear streams, creeks, and springs, to great rivers and lakes, although they sometimes frequent the latter. Where the animals are abundant their dams are thrown across the stream up to its very source, and are formed of small stones, mosses, mud, and branches of trees stripped of their bark, and measuring about three feet in length and from six inches to a foot in circumference. That they frequently fell trees of considerable size is indisputable, on some occasions trunks as large as eighteen inches in diameter have been found, but even with their sharp teeth the labour must be immense, and their only object in undertaking it is to make use of the bark and branches, the latter of which are alone employed in the construction of a dam, the trunk, divested of its bark, being left where it falls. The trappers state that the beavers give them notice of the approach of an early winter by cutting their wood before the usual time ; and indicate pretty accurately its probable severity by the precautions they take to meet its rigour.

In forming their dams the animals employ their noses as a pig does its snout, rooting up mosses and clay, and stuffing them between the framework of matted and interlaced sticks until the whole fabric is completely water-tight, and so firm and compact that even men armed with ice-chisels and such like tools find great difficulty in breaking through them. In height the dams average from seven to nine feet, according to the depth of water, being broad at the base, and the sides sloping inward towards each other, so as to form a narrow platform about two feet wide at the top. The object of these curious structures is that they may possess a sufficient quantity of water at all seasons, and the skill displayed by the animals in the shape of their dams is a triumph of engineering science. If the stream runs gently they throw the barrier boldly athwart it, but if the current rushes past swiftly, and is liable by floods to be converted into a destructive torrent, they build the dam in a crescent form, its convex side opposed to the fury of the stream. Some idea of the extent of these works may be formed when Audubon states that they are sometimes found *three hundred yards* in length, and often extend beyond the bed of the stream in a circular form, so as to overflow all the timber near the margin, which the beavers cut down for food during the winter, heap together in large quantities, and so securely fasten to the shore, under the surface of the water, that even a strong current cannot tear it away. Some of the most fertile patches of land in Canada are due to the beavers. Trees, branches, dead leaves, and stones are borne down by the water and stopped by the dam, which in course of time becomes a solid mass of many acres in extent, clothed with a rich vegetation, and in every way adapted to the farmer, by whom these " beaver meadows " as they are termed, are highly prized.

The houses or "lodges" in which the beavers dwell are as curious as the dam, in the vicinity of which they usually stand. The larger ones are, in the interior, about seven feet in diameter and between two and three feet in height, resembling in fact, a great oven. These are placed either at the edge of, or in the water, and in front of them the beavers scratch away a deep trench, so deep that all fear of the water becoming frozen is removed, and in this the wood mentioned above, as intended for winter food, is stored, and this channel also affords them free access to their dam, should they require to visit it for repairs or any other purpose. The top of the lodge is formed by placing branches of trees matted with moss, mud, grasses, &c., together, until the whole fabric measures on the outside from twelve to twenty feet in diameter, and is six or eight feet high, according to the number of inhabitants. The outer coating is entirely of mud or earth, and smoothed off as if plastered with a trowel, but as they never work by daylight, it is still unknown how they perform this. The mud covering is renewed every year, generally late in the autumn, when frost has set in, and the ingredients becoming frozen in a solid mass add much to the security of, the inmates, protecting them from the wolverene, who, next to man, is their worst enemy.

The furniture of their houses is very simple, consisting only of a bed for each member of the family, formed of grass or the tender bark of young trees, and placed against the side of the lodge, the centre being left unoccupied. Every evening they visit their dam and minutely examine it ; if a log is washed away or displaced the mischief is at once repaired, and fresh material is afforded by the sticks stored for food. These are piled in front of the lodges, and when the animal feels hungry he detaches a stick from the bundle, takes it inside, strips off the bark, on which he feeds at his leisure, and then carries the wood to the dam, should it need repairs, or lets it float away, for the beaver is scrupulously clean, and allows no litter or dirt to accumulate within its abode, being in this respect a model that many of its human enemies might study with advantage.

We now come to a curious phase of beaver life. It seems that amongst their number there are some too lazy and idle to work, to build lodges, repair dams, or in fact, to perform any of the duties of a well-conditioned and industrious member of the community. These scapegraces are very summarily dealt with by their virtuous brethren, who first of all give them a good worrying, cutting off a portion of their tails and otherwise maltreating them, and then turn them out neck and crop into the world to reap the fruits of their improvidence. These wretched outcasts—called Paresseux by the trappers—herd together in gangs of half a dozen or so, and never form a dam, but content themselves with digging a hole from the water which runs obliquely upwards and emerges some twenty or thirty feet from the brink. By this passage the improvident ones sally forth when they are in want of food, and return with a length of wood, whose bark they gnaw off in their *souterrain*. But destruction comes quickly on the heads of the wretched paresseux ; either the trapper or the wolverene find out their passage, and make short work of the whole fraternity one after the other, from which just retribution a very pretty little moral could be deduced, if necessary. Before, however, utterly condemning these lazy beavers, let us remember that perhaps after all their only sin

consists in being physically weaker than their brethren, for the paresseux are always males, and it is
not at all improbable, that, as is common with the
males of many species of animals, they have fought
with rivals, been conquered and driven forth by the
victors, thus taking up the rôle of paresseux more
from necessity than inclination ; and this theory
would satisfactorily account for the marks of
violence they always carry about them.

Beavers are in good condition for the trapper
from September to May in the greater part of
America, though in the Rocky Mountains there is
no close season, the cold causing the coat to remain
thick all the year round.   They are often eaten, the
sides of the belly, the rump, the liver, and the tail
being highly esteemed ; indeed the last-mentioned
memb r is considered a peculiar delicacy, possessing
nearly the taste of beef marrow; but it is so oily that
only a very small quantity can be eaten, and no
stomach less omnivorous than a trapper's could pos-
sibly digest it. At the approach of autumn beavers
become very fat, but fall off gradually during the
winter, so that when spring comes they are little
better than skin and bone. The bark of young
trees, and the white, tender, juicy roots of certain
aquatic plants which are then in season, soon fill them
out again, and they become a great size. Cartwright

mentions finding one that weighed forty-five pounds, and sixty-one pounds before cleaning is mentioned by another traveller ; but both these specimens must have far exceeded the average weight, which may be put down at from fifteen to twenty-five pounds.

Their food consists of the bark of the aspen, willow, birch, poplar, and alder, besides bulbous and other roots. In summer, when they wander to some distance from water, they eat berries, leaves, and various kinds of herbage. The young are born in the months of April and May ; those produced in the latter month are the most valuable, as they grow rapidly, and become large and strong, being unchecked in their growth, as is often the case with those born at an earlier season. The dam usually brings forth from two to five at a time, and the young beavers, whose eyes are open at their birth, remain with their mother for at least a year, and not unfrequently for two. Where food is abundant and they are undisturbed, a family of ten or a dozen may be seen living in one lodge. They are often caught young, and are easily domesticated. And now I think I have taxed the reader's patience sufficiently concerning the *Castor Fiber;* the method in which it is captured will appear further on.

CHAPTER IV.

BOUT a week after Paul Gresham's arrival at Osnaburg House, he was standing talking to Mr. Groves and Pierre Lefranc at the main gate of the enclosure, when the latter broke off in the middle of a sentence and gazed intently in the direction of the lake that lay spread before them, calm, clear and beautiful, its surface broken by numerous little islands whose light green foliage formed a contrast to the gloomy pines, and reminded the beholder of emeralds in an azure setting.

"Monsieur Groves, I see three—four canoe— I think the Ojibbeways sall come at last with their peltries," quoth Pierre, after a keen scrutiny. And running back to the house for his glass, Paul distinctly saw several canoes threading their way amongst the distant islands, but such mere specks that no eyes less sharp than a trapper's would have discerned their approach.

" Well, thank goodness they are coming at last,"

said Groves, with visible satisfaction, "for when they have gone we shall be able to roam about a little, and get some shooting. The cunning rascals," he added, "they knew well enough that fresh stores had reached the house some days ago, and have only kept away to tantalise us, and lead us to suppose that they had gone to some rival trader. They will now make a great favour of trading with the Company, and will demand all sorts of presents. They are a pretty deep lot, whatever people may say; are they not, Pierre?"

"*Il y a*, there is von Ojeeb chief, who have cheat me of my traps *il y a deux ans*, two year past. *Il s'appelle Tête-de-bois*, suppose he come here, I shall beat his head of wood."

"Well, don't commence hostilities until we have got all the skins," said Groves, laughing. "But come along, we must get ready to receive them with due honours."

At Osnaburg House there were only five men besides the officer in charge, namely, three labourers, an interpreter, and a postmaster. What on earth can a postmaster do at a place where letters only arrive twice or thrice a year? will be the first question the reader puts to himself, and to answer it satisfactorily I must state that there are six grades in the Hudson's Bay Company's service.

Lowest in the scale are the labourers, generally French Canadians, half-breeds, or Orkneymen; indeed the great majority of the Company's servants are Scotch. These men are always employed, although their occupations necessarily vary according to the season. In the autumn they cut up and store the large quantity of fuel that will be required when the frost sets in; in the summer they fish, and transport the peltry from their post to the nearest depôt; in fact, they make themselves generally useful, and they are ready to turn their hands to anything, from trapping a beaver to repairing the stockade, or shovelling away the drift snow in the winter. Next in rank to the labourers are the interpreters. The latter are usually selected from the most intelligent labourers, who, from being long acquainted with the Indians, have picked up their language sufficiently to entitle them to the higher grade. They are a most useful, trustworthy body of men, and from their ranks are drawn the postmasters who have made themselves conspicuous for activity and intelligence. The postmaster ranks with the gentlemen of the service, with whom he lives and takes his meals, and he is often placed in charge of a small station, from whence he derives his name, which signifies "master of a post," and has nothing to do with letter-boxes, stamps, **or** telegrams. The above-mentioned grades are all filled by members of the working classes. Now come the young men of birth and education, who enter the Company's service at an early age as apprentice clerks, in which capacity they serve for five years, at the end of which they are sufficiently conversant with their duty to drop the apprentice and become clerks. After about fifteen years' service, the clerk becomes a half-shareholder, and is then termed a chief trader; in due course he becomes a whole-shareholder, and has then reached the top of the tree, changing his appellation for the last time to that of chief factor.

In obedience to Mr. Groves' orders, the men all furbished up their weapons, and loaded the old swivels with reduced blank charges; the gate was then closed, the English ensign run up to the flag-staff, and the inmates of the fort awaited the arrival of the canoes, which were now rapidly nearing the shore. Soon the prow of the foremost one grated on the sand, and its occupants, consisting of two Ojibbeway hunters and their squaws, stepped upon the shore, the latter proceeding to land the parcels of furs, while their better halves walked up to the wicket of the gate, where Groves and his interpreter stood ready to welcome them. The parley was of short duration, for both sides were equally anxious to come to business, and soon the gate was thrown open, and the Indians entered to the number of eighteen, for the other canoes had arrived within a few minutes of the first one. Paul looked with the utmost curiosity at these children of the forest, who showed none of the taciturnity and sullen reserve that his book-lore on the subject had led him to expect. They shook hands with Groves, Pierre, and such others of the white men as were known to them, and joyfully accepted the invitation from the officer to smoke and lighten their hearts with a little rum. Neither was the dress of the Ojibbeways such as Paul had anticipated ; they wore deer-skins and moccasins it is true, but their attire had none of the flowing grace that he had always imagined was the distinctive element in an Indian toilette. The fact was that he had forgotten that he was amongst the Wood Indians, and not their brethren of the plains and prairies. The latter are always mounted, and therefore the tufts. of hair and other finery that adorns their persons is no impediment to their movements, whereas, if a Wood Indian indulged in such vanities he would be hung up in every bush, and would stand but a poor chance of stealing silently upon deer or any other game.

A large building had been held in readiness for the arrival of the Indians, and thither they all repaired, preceded by Mr. Groves, Paul, Pierre, and the interpreter. The white men seated themselves on buffalo robes, and their guests formed a circle, around which the pipe lighted by the officer passed solemnly, each man taking a long whiff and handing it to his neighbour, after which he allowed the smoke to roll out slowly from his mouth and nostrils. Whilst this important ceremony was proceeding, perfect silence reigned throughout the assembly; but after the rum had passed round once or twice all restraint was removed, and conversation went on freely enough by means of signs and broken English and French.

" Monsieur Paul," whispered Lefranc, as two new Indians joined the circle, " *voyez-vous ces hommes ? L'un, le plus grand*—the vary big one, that is *Tête-de-bois*, the rascal who steal my traps."

Paul looked at the new-comer, and saw an Ojibbeway of gigantic size, and with rather sinister features, the effect perhaps of a scar which traversed the countenance from the eye to the chin. *Tête-de-bois* took his seat among the rest of his tribe, who made way with alacrity, for he was held in great respect, owing to his enormous strength. He took no notice of Pierre, pretending not to see him, and applied himself steadily to the rum bottle whenever it came within his reach. Meanwhile

F

the squaws were unloading the canoes and carrying the furs up to the fort.

After a couple of hours had been consumed in the Council Chamber, the party broke up at a signal from Mr. Groves, and the swivels having been fired to intimate that business had commenced, the whole party trooped into the trading house, accompanied by the squaws, who each carried a bundle of furs. Whether *Tête-de-bois* thought that Pierre had forgotten all about the traps, I know not, but appearing to recognise him for the first time, the Indian approached the Canadian with outstretched hand. This was more than honest Pierre could stand, and he dashed the Chief's arm aside with a volley of mingled French, Indian, and English expletives that I must be pardoned for not inserting here. The latter turned an ashy gray colour at the insult, though he only smiled and said, " My brother has taken too much fire-water," yet those best aquainted with the Indian character knew that the trapper had made a deadly and unscrupulous enemy, and none better than Pierre himself, who laughed the warnings of his friends to scorn, saying that he was quite old and ugly enough to take care of himself.

And now commenced the trading. The building in which this took place was an ample wooden edifice termed the "store," in which was to be found every conceivable article that the reader can imagine, anything, in short, "from a penny whistle to a sheet anchor" as a sailor would say. The Indians advanced one by one to a counter behind which were stationed Mr. Groves, Paul, and the interpreter. Each man was accompanied by his squaw, who carried one or more bundles of furs, which were placed on the counter, spread out, and carefully examined. Mr. Groves then made them up into bundles, and handed the owner a number of little pieces of wood, each of which signified the value of a beaver skin, or castor, as it is termed in some parts of the territory. This is the recognised standard valuation, and according to it everything is reckoned, for cash is utterly unknown. A bear-skin is worth so many beaver-skins, a marten's skin worth so many, and the whole having been assorted and valued in the presence of the hunter, the equivalent number of pieces of wood are made over to him, and he can purchase whatever he pleases, handing back the wooden labels as payment until his store is exhausted. The Indians watch the counting and the process of valuing with the keenest interest, and strive to drive the hardest bargains possible, but as the castor only represents a purchasing power of from one to two shillings, and the articles they need are sold at a very high price, the Company realise an enormous profit.

But it must be remembered that the labour and expense of getting stores up to these lonely places is excessive. Captain Butler puts the whole case so clearly before the reader that I venture to quote the following passage from his admirable book. He says : " That rough flint gun, which might have done duty in the days of the Stuarts, is worth many a rich sable in the country of the Dogribs and the Loucheaux, and is bartered for skins whose value can be rated at four times their weight in gold ; but the gun on the banks of the Thames, and the gun in the pine woods of the Mackenzie are two widely different articles. The old rough flint, whose bent barrel the Indians will often straighten between the cleft of a tree or in the crevice of a rock, has been made precious by the long labour of many men, by the trackless wastes through which it has been carried, by winter-famine of those who have to vend it, by the years which elapse between its departure from the workshop and the return of that skin of sable or silver fox for which it has been bartered. They are short-sighted men who hold that because the flint gun and the sable possess such different values in London, these articles should also possess their relative values in North America, and argue from this that the Hudson's Bay Company treat the Indians unfairly; they are short-sighted men, I say, and know not of what they speak. That old rough flint has often cost more to put in the hands of that Dogrib hunter than the best finished central-fire of Boss or Purdey."

In the selection of articles in exchange for his furs the Indian is often sorely puzzled; he sees around him many coloured blankets, gaudy chintzes, and calicoes such as his heart loveth, and much tobacco, without which he can hardly be said to exist. His vanity prompts him to exchange his castors against such finery, though prudence whispers audibly that the bitter winter is drawing nigh apace, and that it were better to prepare for its vigour by the purchase of warm clothing and new steel traps. In this state of indecision the influence of a favourite squaw is often all-powerful for good or evil; if she is prudent the castors will be profitably laid out, if not, the reverse will take place, and a few yards of coloured ribbon, chintz, and beads will be all the hunter has to show in return for many months hard and dangerous work.

After the trading was finished for the night, the Indians withdrew to the shores of the lake, where their squaws had built rough shelters of pine-boughs, under which they retired to contemplate

their new purchases by the light of the fire, and,
if they have any castors left, to talk over how they
should be expended on the morrow.   Such is the
method in which the fur trade is carried on at the
Hudson's Bay stations among the Wood Indians.
From constant intercourse with Europeans these
people may be regarded as semi-civilised, and little
danger need be apprehended from them.   But in
the more remote stations on the prairies and
beyond the Rocky Mountains on the wild Columbia
River, matters are differently arranged : that is to
say, that though the mode of trade is precisely
similar, the castor still being the unit of com-
putation and the process of barter exactly as I
have described above, stringent precautions are
taken for the safety of the fort and its occupants.
Instead of arriving in small numbers, the warlike
Blackfeet or Crees visit the fort in large troops
and fully armed ; for to reach it they often have
to pass through an enemy's country, where a fierce
conflict is at any moment imminent.   Mounted on
their half-broken mustangs, the warriors approach
the station, which is not only more strongly built
than Osnaburg House, but is also in good repair,
and garrisoned with sufficient men to defeat any
sudden attempt.   Each rider leads another horse, on
which is packed his stock of peltry, and on arriving

at a distance of a couple of hundred yards from the fort, the cavalcade reins up, while the chief rides forward to meet the factor. Presents are commonly exchanged, and many complimentary speeches passed, after which business commences. But the Indians are not permitted to enter the trading room indiscriminately, neither are the gaudy chintzes and beads submitted to their view, for, at sight of such marvellous riches, their wish to possess them would prove uncontrollable, and a disturbance would probably break out. The trading room in these stations is so constructed that all communication between it and the surrounding buildings can be cut off, and to prevent too many Indians crowding in it is so contrived that they have to pass through a long narrow passage, of only suffi-cient width to admit one at a time, the passage being built at an acute angle to the window at which the factor stands, so that the savages are unable to shoot him, as they could were it made perfectly straight. The furs obtained by barter are packed away in an underground chamber concealed beneath the large table in the factor's room, and this apartment has somebody in it night and day, so that theft is rendered impossible unless the station is regularly attacked and sacked. Once a year the furs are made up into parcels and transported to the nearest depôt, for transhipment to England. Whenever possible this is effected by water, and during the summer months numerous brigades of canoes are constantly passing up and down the rivers running into Hudson Bay, taking down the peltries and returning with stores. Where water carriage is unavailable, pack-horses are employed.

In less than a week the Ojibbeways had parted with all their peltries, and left for the opposite side of the lake, their canoes laden with blankets, woollen clothing, and other articles that have become necessary to the red man since the trader has taught him their use. No further collision had taken place between Pierre Lefranc and the chief, and the whole matter was speedily forgotten by all but the Canadian's little Cree wife, who stoutly maintained that *Tête-de-bois* meditated revenge, and recommended her husband to make matters smooth by shooting the chief, at which suggestion the jovial Frenchman burst into a huge laugh, and told his better half to stick to her pots and pans, and leave him to take care of himself.

"Now, Gresham," said Mr. Groves, as the two young men sat smoking before the stove after supper, for the nights were now a little chilly, "we can get some shooting, for there will be no more trade this year. Suppose we send for Pierre and talk it over."

The Canadian was accordingly summoned, and a long consultation held, which resulted in several minor expeditions, the particulars of which are hardly worth recording. A few deer were shot, and plenty of wild fowl, but by Pierre's advice the grand hunt was postponed until the winter had set well in, when the snow would be upon the ground, and they could seek for moose with some chance of success.

And thus the autumn passed away, and the falling mercury indicated the approach of winter. Did Paul Gresham feel dull thus shut up with only two companions? the reader will ask. No, the whole life was too novel to admit the inroads of *ennui.* Whether in-doors or out there was always something that required looking to, and dullness, the offspring of idleness, found no loop-hole by which it could enter. At last the few days of genial weather that precede the cold, and are known as the Indian summer, came to a close, and with a sudden bound the winter came upon them. When Paul went to bed the air was still and serene, the party-coloured leaves hung tremblingly on the boughs in all the wondrous beauty of their autumn tints; when he awoke in the morning a widely different scene presented itself. The leaves were whirling madly in the air, borne aloft by a blast that shook old Osnaburg House to its foundations, and churned the usually placid lake into a yeast of angry white ; the little islands that the preceding night had looked so beautiful as the setting sun threw into relief their varied hues, were now little black spots half buried in the flying scud ; the gloomy pines creaked and moaned dismally as the blast swayed them to and fro, the aspect of the country was changed as by the touch of an enchanter's wand. But the storm speedily subsided, and down came the snow, in little granules at first, but presently in broad, crisp flakes, that in two hours flung a white mantle over the whole country. Down it came noiselessly but ceaselessly, for hour after hour, for day after day, until a week had run its course, then the leaden sky broke into rifts through which the bright sun smiled cheerily, the discomforted snow clouds fled away and vanished in the distance, the pure blue canopy appeared illimitable in its serene tranquillity, and the bright stars shone radiant through the frosty air, seeming so close that the beholder felt impelled to stretch out his hands and grasp them. The winter had set in ; the hard, rigorous, unyielding cold of Canada, so different to the changeable climate and the noxious east winds of

England, on whose hateful wings are too often borne rheumatism, consumption—death.

" Rise, rise, *Messieurs*," shouted Pierre, entering the room in which the two young men were coiled up under a load of buffalo robes and blankets, "you must rise, *c'est le point de jour.*"

Turning out in such weather is not the pleasantest part of the day's work, but both Paul and his friend were fully aware that like most disagreeable things the more you look at them the less you like them, so with a bound they sprang to their feet, and in due time joined the Canadian, who was busily employed at the stove frying some venison collops and making tea for breakfast, not the weak infusion that we sip in England, but a good black beverage, strong enough, in Canadian parlance, "to float an axe." Perhaps the reader would like to know in what manner of garment our friends have arrayed themselves to withstand the biting cold. Both the young men are dressed alike, so the description of one will apply to both. Mr. Groves has thrust his extremities into a pair of buck-skin trousers, under which are warm woollen drawers. On his feet are dragged successively three pairs of socks, made out of stout blanketing, outside of which are fastened a pair of moose-skin moccasins tied firmly round the ankle. It is perhaps needless to state that moccasins

are rough foot coverings made from the skin of some
wild animal, and worn by the Indians as we wear boots.
An Ojibbeway would, however, ascend a hill thus
shod that a white man would be unable to get half-
way up without great pain and inconvenience. The
truth is that the moccasin is adapted to the Indian
only, owing to the peculiar conformation of his foot,
which has much shorter toes. For a European,
whose soles are soft and who has no prehensile
power in his feet, moccasins are a snare and a
delusion, except in two certain cases. When travelling with dog-sleighs or walking on snow-shoes
they are invaluable, on any other occasion a pair of
nailed lace-up boots are far preferable. Our friends
were to use snow-shoes, and therefore Mr. Groves
donned moose-skin moccasins, over which he hauled
a pair of strong cloth leggings in a measure for
warmth, but chiefly to prevent snow adhering to the
buck-skins. Over several flannel shirts and under
waistcoats came a capote made of deer-skin, and
lined throughout with fur, and this garment was
confined at the waist by a belt, at which hung his
ammunition, hunting knife, fire-bag, and other
little necessaries. A fur boa was wrapped round
his neck, a cap with ear-flaps of similar material
adorned his head, and an immense pair of
duffle mittens covered with buck-skin dangled by

a woollen cord from his neck and completed the equipment.

The steaming venison rashers soon disappeared beneath the action of three powerful pairs of jaws, and long ere the bright morning star had paled and disappeared beneath the golden shafts of the rising sun, the hunters had quitted the table, and stepped into the two sleighs awaiting them outside.

94

CHAPTER V.

HEERILY tinkled the bells as the sleighs, each drawn by a couple of horses, sped over the smooth snow-covered ice. Our friends had started on their long projected expedition, and the country judged most likely to carry moose lay on the further side of the lake, and thither the party proceeded in their sleighs, which were to be driven back to Osnaburg House by two of the labourers, who accompanied them for that purpose. And whilst they glide merrily over the frozen surface, the breath pouring in clouds from their mouths and forming great pear-shaped icicles in Pierre's bushy beard, let us take a glance at the animal they are about to hunt.

The Moose or Elk (*Cervus Alces*) is the largest of any known species of deer, and requires to be seen in its native forests before its majestic stature and imposing appearance can be thoroughly realised; for, owing to the apparent disproportion of its limbs, the animal has a clumsy, uncouth look, which is much more remarkable in a state of captivity than when it wanders at will in the gloomy pine woods of North America. The head of the moose much resembles that of an enormous jackass, being very long, and having a prehensile muzzle, which extends several inches beyond the lower lip. The nostrils are narrow and long; the eyes small in proportion to the head, and the ears of considerable length. The neck is very short, and is surmounted by a compact mane of coarse hairs, which the animal erects when excited or enraged. But the wondrous part of the moose are its horns, which are very large and palmated at the extremities, and Audubon mentions the curious fact that the palms on the main branches of the horns not only differ in different individuals, but do not often correspond on the head of the same animal. A single pair of antlers sometimes reach the enormous weight of over sixty pounds. The colour of the moose varies according to its age, and the upper portion of its body is darker than the under. The young animals for the first winter are of a reddish-brown colour, but as they advance in years the coat deepens in hue until it becomes nearly black, from whence it is named by one naturalist the "American Black Elk."

Formerly moose were very abundant in Canada, but the hunter has followed them up perseveringly, and their numbers are much diminished. In the summer they frequent the vicinities of rivers and lakes, not only to escape the attacks of insects by plunging into the water, where only their noses and horns appear above the surface, but also to avoid injuring their antlers, which during their growth are very soft and sensitive. Here also the moose finds abundant provision, feeding on the water plants, or browsing on the trees fringing the shore. In the winter they retire to the wooded mountain ridges, and associate together in groups of three, four or even more, beating down the snow with their hoofs, and forming what are known as "yards," which are generally found on the slope facing the south, where there is abundance of maple and of other hard-wood trees upon which they feed, either by browsing on the tender twigs or peeling the bark from the stems of such as are only three or four inches in diameter. Though not so long as the giraffe's, their pendulous upper lip is admirably adapted for grasping and pulling down the branches, whilst they peel off the bark by scraping upwards with their sharp gouge-like teeth, and thus denude the tree to the height of seven or eight feet from the surface of the snow. When every tree in the neighbourhood of a "yard" has been stripped, the moose will leave it; but so averse

THE ENCAMPMENT OF GROVES AND PAUL ON THE MOOSE EXPEDITION.

Page 97.

are they to moving, that they will break branches as large as a man's thigh sooner than shift to another place where food is plentiful. The hunter ascertains whether the moose has been recently in its "yard" by scraping away the surface of the snow from the trees already stripped, and if they have been barked *below* the snow the animal has left the spot for some time, and its trail is not worth following.

Mr. Kendall, of the Literary Society of Quebec, speaks thus of the wonderful horns of the moose : "The antlers begin to sprout in April, and at first appear like two black knobs. They complete their growth in July, when the skin which covers them peels off and leaves them perfectly white ; exposure to the sun and air, however, soon renders them brown. When we consider the immense size to which some of them grow in such a short period of time, it seems almost incredible that two such enormous excresences could be deposited from the circulating system alone ; the daily growth is distinctly marked on the velvety covering by a light shade carried around them. The first year the antlers are only about one inch long, the second year, four or five inches, with perhaps the rudiment of a point, the third year about nine inches, when each divides into a fork still round in

G

form, the fourth year they become palmated, with a brow antler and three or four points, the fiftn season they have two crown antlers and perhaps five points, the points increasing in size each year, and one or two points being added annually, until the animal arrives at its greatest vigour, after which period they decrease in size, and the points are not so fully thrown out. The longest pair I ever met with had eighteen points (others have seen them with twenty-three points), they expanded five feet nine inches to the outside of the tips; the breadth of palm eleven inches without the points; circumference of shaft, clear of the burr, nine inches; weight, seventy pounds! The old and vigorous animals invariably shed them in December; some, of four or five years old, I have known to carry them as late as March, but this is not often the case."

By noon the sleighs have reached the further side of the lake and deposited the hunters at the spot selected for their camp. This is at a short distance only from the water, and while Pierre Lefranc starts off on his snow-shoes to search for any "sign" of moose, Groves and Paul see to the encampment, and then go down to the lake to catch a dish of fresh fish. And let us see how the hunters try to make themselves a comfortable night's lodging in that piercing cold. First a fine tree is selected, a huge giant whose towering crest has overlooked Lake Joseph for three centuries at least, and whose trunk is free from brushwood at the base, whilst his spreading branches will form a good shelter should it come on suddenly to snow. Using their snow-shoes as shovels, the two young men proceed to clear away a space several yards in diameter, piling the snow at the edge of the circular clearing as a wall, and the ground being covered to the depth of over three feet, this snow barrier is seven feet high by the time that they have finished.

And let me here remark that the Canadian snow differs greatly from the moist stuff to which we are accustomed in England. Owing to the intense cold the Canadian snow is crisp, dry, and light—so light that a much greater quantity of it is requisite to produce an inch of water, than would be required in Great Britain.

Taking their axes the young men next fell a fir tree, and one lops off its branches while the other drags them to the clearing and strews the ground thickly with the fragrant shoots. The trunk is next "logged off" into lengths of about five feet, and a roaring fire soon blazes at the foot of the old pine. While Groves is felling another tree,

for it would never do to run short of firewood in
the night, Paul descends to the lake for water, and
soon returns with a bucket full, but to obtain it he
has had to break open the ice with his ice-axe, and
the exposed surface freezes before he can reach the
camp.

And now while Groves boils the kettle and fries
a little venison, Paul goes again to the lake to catch
a dish of fish. Let us see how he sets about it.
First of all he scrapes away the snow with his shoe,
and having laid bare a portion of the ice proceeds
to chop a hole in it with his axe. In about ten
minutes the unfrozen water is reached, and the hole
enlarged until it is a couple of feet square. Paul
now puts a piece of raw venison on his hook, which
is of considerable size, and fastened to a thick,
strong line, and drops it into the hole, first tying a
long bough at the end of the line, so that a heavy
fish cannot pull it into the water, for the cold is too
intense to permit of his sitting down and fishing
according to our acceptation of the term ; if he did
anything half so foolish, he would infallibly be
frost-bitten, and lose a toe or two, or perhaps his
nose. Not caring for either of these contingencies,
Paul walks briskly about, but his patience is not
long tried, for in less than five minutes the line
runs violently out, and he hauls up a fine bream

and flings him upon the ice, to flap about for
a short time before becoming frozen as hard as a
board, and so he goes on until a shout from Groves
warns him that if he expects to find any venison
in the pan he had better hurry back. Fish are
exceedingly plentiful in the Hudson Bay Territory,
and Lord Milton and Doctor Cheadle mention the
following curious circumstance:—"The lake was
about half a mile in length, and of nearly equal
breadth, but of no great depth. The water had
seemingly frozen to the bottom, except at one end,
where a spring bubbled up, and a hole of about a
yard in diameter existed in the covering of ice,
which was there only a few inches thick. The
water in this hole was crowded with myriads of
small fish, most of them not much larger than a
man's finger, and so closely packed that they could
not move freely. On thrusting in an arm, it seemed
like plunging it into a mass of thick stirabout.
The snow was beaten down all round hard and
level as a road, by the numbers of animals which
flocked to the Lenten feast. Tracks converged
from every side. Here were the foot-prints of the
cross or silver fox, delicately impressed in the snow
as he trotted daintily along with light and airy
tread ; the rough marks of the clumsier fisher ; the
clear, sharply defined track of the active mink ;

and the great coarse trail of the ever-galloping, ubiquitous wolverene. Scores of crows perched on the trees around, sleepily digesting their frequent meals. Judging by the state of the snow and collection of dung the consumption must have gone on for weeks, yet the supply seemed as plentiful as ever."

Split open or boiled over the fire by means of two sticks for handles, a fine fresh fish is a great delicacy, and our friends were proceeding to enjoy their supper when a shout in the distance announced that Pierre Lefranc was on his way back. Paul slipped on his snow-shoes and advanced to meet him, and was highly delighted to learn that a moose "yard" had been found within a short distance and the "sign" showed plainly that it was still frequented. Whilst Paul was stooping down to play with the dogs that had accompanied the trapper, he caught a glimpse of the camp, and heedless of the cold, stood for a few minutes in silent admiration. Night had fallen, and the fresh logs heaped on by Groves to welcome the Canadian threw up sheets of ruddy flame, that roared in the pine branches above them and sent upward a million of sparks that coruscated far overhead before disappearing for ever. The pure sheeting with which the earth was covered flashed back the light of the fire as though the ground were thickly sprinkled with seed diamonds, while the trunks of the trees caught a ruby hue, and the snow became tinged with a delicate sea-shell pink of exquisite beauty. Those who have seen some of the marvellous fairy transformation scenes in our Christmas pantomimes can, perhaps, form some idea of the sight now presented to Paul's admiring gaze, but in the former all is false and the heavy atmosphere tainted with gas, whilst here the air was dry and exhilarating, and nature needed no sulphurous chemicals to throw a magic splendour on the landscape.

Pierre was in high spirits, and if a good appetite waits only on a light heart, his breast must have been singularly free from "carking care," for the venison and fish vanished before his powerful jaws with a rapidity that excited first the admiration then the wonder of the beholders. As he ate he kept up a running conversation, or perhaps it would be more correct to say a steady fire of remarks, for both the young men sat still listening and never opening their lips.

"*Quatre* moose, monsieur, two big vons, a bull and a cow, and two *petites*—how you call it?— calves. And I have see plenty tracks of marten, and the trail of von big bear. Oh, if Monsieur Tanner was only here for de hont!" and so on until his appetite was at length appeased, and after a pipe, the fire was finally replenished, and the whole party rolling themselves in their buffalo robes sank into a profound slumber.

Before dawn the camp was astir, jorums of smoking tea hastily swallowed, dried venison steaks disposed of, the caps on their guns replaced—almost a needless precaution in that dry atmosphere, and slipping their feet into snow-shoes the three men started off into the wilderness.

I have mentioned snow-shoes several times, and now seems the proper time to describe these useful articles and the manner of wearing them. The object of the snow shoe is to present a broad surface to the snow, and prevent the hunter sinking up to his middle at each step, which would totally exhaust his strength in a few hundred yards. It varies in dimensions according to the condition of the snow and the taste of the wearer, but a little under four feet in length by one foot in breadth is a fair average. It consists of a light framework formed of two pieces of hard, tough wood, which are securely fastened together at either end, and spread out near the middle by wooden bars, which give support to the frame and cause it to assume an oval form. The whole of the interior is then filled up with a network of hide thongs, very much like a tennis bat, in which a small hole is left towards the 'ore part of the shoe. On this network the foot of the hunter rests, and the hole plays a most im- portant part, for over it come the toes and in it they find room to play. A proficient in the use of snow-shoes will never stoop down to tie them on, but will twist his foot into the loops provided for that purpose, and walk away. On advancing the foot the shoe rests on the upper part just where the toes articulate (or spring out), these members passing through the hole above mentioned ; and when the stride is completed and the advanced foot planted on the ground to bring up the other, the shoe slips off the toes which dragged it forward, and rests firmly on the lattice work. And now the use of the hole is apparent, for without it the toes would be bent upwards at each step, and would soon be- come cramped and stiff, or even raw if the novice persisted in travelling. To gain the knack of dropping and catching up the shoe at each stride a great deal of practice is requisite, and the art can only be learned on snow itself, for the earth would not permit the toes to sink through the hole. We live, however, in an age of progress. The " rink" has rendered skating possible at midsummer, and who knows if some ingenious speculator may not start an establishment where the youth of England may acquire the graceful art of swinging along on snow shoes ? Flour would form an admirable substitute for snow, and the beginners would carry on their coats the story of their mishaps. As the latter would be very frequent, and dives into the flour of momentary occurrence, may I be permitted to suggest that its proprietor should call his establishment, when he starts it, by a name at once appropriate and euphonious—the " Sink."

In walking on snow-shoes they are never lifted entirely clear of the surface, but the hind parts are permitted to trail, leaving a mark upon the snow by which the novice can be immediately distinguished from the proficient. The former leaves a wavy, irregular line, sometimes of considerable depth, at others barely grazing it, whereas the trail of the latter is uniform and undeviating. Notwithstanding their great size these shoes are very light, and a man accustomed to their use can cover thirty miles a day without difficulty. Frosty weather is the easiest to travel in, as the snow is fine and falls through the network without sticking, if the weather be warm and the snow melting, it clogs the shoe, renders it heavy, and soon galls the feet.

From the above description their use will, doubtless, seem easy enough, but an attempt to walk in them will soon alter this opinion. The novice does not remember their width, and, planting one on the top of the other, comes headlong to the ground. Even experienced hunters are sometimes thrown down by their dog stepping on the heel of the shoe, but a few sound thrashings render the animal cautious. I mentioned a little further back that Pierre was accompanied by two or three dogs, but this was too high-sounding a name to bestow on the wretched little curs that are used in moose hunting, not to seize and drag down the prey, but simply to worry him by snapping at his heels. The smaller they are in size the better, as they are then enabled to run upon the surface of the snow without breaking through the crust.

Paul had devoted all his leisure moments at Osnaburg House to practising on snow-shoes, and had become quite sufficiently expert to walk without difficulty. His length of limb gave him a considerable advantage, for a long, swinging stride is of great consequence. So they walked onwards for several miles, the Canadian leading the way and following his tracks of the previous night. Many hares and grouse were seen, but for fear of alarming the nobler game, were allowed to pass unheeded. Pierre, however, pointed out the track of a wolf, and vowed to trap it before he returned to the house. At length the vicinity of the "yard," was reached, but a light breeze having sprung up, the Canadian counselled a detour for the purpose of approaching the game from the lee side, and by the time this was accomplished it was high noon. A halt was then called, and the hunter delivered his instructions, which I shall render into English in place of transcribing his curious jargon of mixed languages. All three men were to creep up cautiously and take their chance of getting a shot at the animals before they detected an enemy's presence. If, however, the moose winded them and made off, they were to follow with all speed; and should the animals separate, Groves, as a more experienced woodsman, was to pursue the right-hand trail, while Pierre Lefranc and Paul, whom the Canadian considered under his especial safe-guard, would follow up the other. From the "sign" on the previous day Pierre felt pretty certain that there were only two full-grown moose in the "yard," and by this arrangement they stood every chance of securing them both. The rendezvous was fixed at the encampment on the following evening, for perhaps one party might be compelled to sleep on the trail.

Noiselessly and carefully the hunters advanced, the dogs keeping in the rear, and the utmost pre-cautions were taken to avoid snapping a twig, or making the faintest sound of any kind, for the moose is endowed with the keenest sense of smell and hearing. Pierre pointed silently to the trees as they stole onward, and Paul saw that they had been quite recently stripped of their bark, the marks of the teeth being plainly visible in the younger trunks. At length the Canadian stopped, and pointed through an opening in the undergrowth. Trembling with excitement Paul looked in the direction indicated, and saw a huge bull moose, as big as a horse, browsing on the young boughs of the tree beneath which he stood.

" Fire," whispered Pierre, " aim behind the shoulder."

The young man raised his gun, covered the mighty beast, and the report rang through the forest, followed immediately by the crashing and splintering of boughs as the affrighted animals tore their way through the undergrowth.

" *En avant! en avant!*" shouted the hunter to his dogs, who instantly dashed forward, and all three men were soon in hot pursuit.

" *Du sang, beaucoup de sang,*" cried the Canadian, on reaching the spot where the moose had first been seen ; " you hit him, Monsieur Paul, very fine. Let us show *grande vitesse*—great hurry, and catch him quick."

It was one thing to talk about hurrying, but quite another to accomplish it, for the moose had selected the worst route possible, and the hunters were impeded at every step by tangled thickets and boughs of fallen trees, over or through which the moose from their great strength made their way with ease and rapidity. When running away from danger the moose always adopt the same method ; the male leads, breaking the way for the others, who follow in his tracks so exactly that it appears as though only one had passed. In case of meeting with an obstacle they are unable to overcome, the herd branch off and reunite, if possible, further on. Such happened in the present instance, for a huge tree, fallen through old age, lying directly in the path of the animals, they divided into two parties, the wounded bull taking to the left, whilst the cow and calves turned off to the right.

"Good-bye, Paul," shouted Groves, as according to the arrangement he followed the latter, "you need not expect to see me back in camp to-night, for I shall follow up the game until I bag them all three. Good luck, old fellow," and waving his hand in token of farewell, he disappeared in the undergrowth.

"*Venez donc*, come along, Monsieur Paul, the moose very much bleed, he not far off."

But Pierre was in error, the wounded bull was a very long way off, and it was almost dusk when they reached the spot where the yelping of the curs announced that he had at last been brought to bay.

"*Prenez garde, monsieur,*" said Pierre, as the young man hurried forward towards the moose, who was now seen standing with his hind quarters against a fallen tree, and striking out furiously with his fore feet at the mongrels. "*Ils sont très dangereux.*"

Here a yell of agony from one of the dogs announced that it had ventured too near the fatal hoof, over and over for five or six yards it rolled, and then lay howling with a broken back.

"*Gardez-vous,*" shouted the hunter, "*il avance!*"

It was too true ; summoning all its strength, the bull dashed forward at the young man who was in advance of his companion. He tried to gain the friendly shelter of a tree, and would probably have succeeded, had not one of the mongrels, in its hurry to escape, trod upon the heel of his snow-shoe, and he fell heavily to the ground. He saw the giant form of the enraged animal towering above him, its hoof raised to strike—another instant and his brains would have been scattered on the trampled snow, when the report of Pierre's gun echoed through the forest, and the huge brute toppled over half burying him in its fall.

" *Etes-vous blessé?* are you hurt?" cried the Canadian in a tone of great alarm as he dragged aside the carcase sufficiently to release the prisoner.

" No, thank you, old fellow, I am all right enough," said Paul, gaining his feet with some difficulty, for snow-shoes are not the best things to practise gymnastics in ; "but it is solely owing to you that I am standing here now."

" Vat should I say to Monsieur Tanner, suppose you not come back safe, eh ? "

" You may rely upon my telling him how much I am indebted to you," replied Paul, "many a man would have sought his own safety, and left me to my fate when he saw that savage brute within four yards of him. What a monster it is," he continued, gazing at the bull, whose throat Pierre had just cut.

The wounded dog was then examined, but its spine was too severely injured to allow of its re-covery, and Pierre despatched it with the other barrel of his gun ; they then set to work skinning the moose, a task they had to accomplish as best they could by moonlight, and having secured the heart, liver, marrow-bones, upper lip, and a good piece of meat, they started for camp, which, owing to the course taken by the wounded bull, was fortunately close at hand.

"What in the world are you going to do with that thing?" asked Paul, as he watched the Canadian washing and cleansing the snout.

"Ah, Monsieur Paul, you not know von good ting, de *moufle* it is *très délicieuse.*"

"You don't mean to eat it, surely?"

"Monsieur shall see," and Pierre applied himself afresh to the preparation of his delicacy, which he eventually put into a saucepan, from whence issued, in time, a most savoury odour. When it was eventually drawn forth, and Paul found that it was a rich, juicy, gelatinous substance, not at all unlike the green fat of the turtle, he quickly changed his opinion, and made his supper chiefly off the dainty he had so lately despised. Before they had finished the meal a long howl was heard in the woods which startled Paul, who was listening eagerly for any signs of Groves' return, and made him anxiously ask the hunter its meaning.

"*C'est un loup*, a rascal wolf, Monsieur Paul, and to-morrow I shall set my traps to catch him by the feets. He is call his compatriots to *manger* the moose."

"Are they at all likely to hurt Mr. Groves?" asked the young man, anxiously.

"No, never fear; they are not yet enough hungry."

This sounded rather cold comfort to Paul, who thought that he should hardly like to come across their path on a dark night ; but he said nothing, and when supper was finished and they were smoking their pipes, he asked the Canadian to tell him a story, the which request honest Pierre was nothing loath to comply with.

"All my own stories, I have already told. But *mon père* he tell me of a voyage he make to Oregon, for the Americans. Suppose you like to hear that, I shall tell it *avec beaucoup de plaisir.*"

"What!" cried Paul, "was your father in Jacob Astor's Company?"

"*Oui, monsieur.*"

"By Jove! I have been hoping to meet somebody who could tell me all about that unfortunate affair for years. You must give me all the particulars, Pierre, and we have plenty of time, for we must have some moose venison ready cooked for Mr. Groves if he returns. Besides, we couldn't sleep with all those wolves baying at the moon, so tell me the story from beginning to end."

The good-natured giant filled up his pipe, lighted it, threw a couple of fresh logs on the fire, and thus commenced. I may add that he spoke in unmixed French when telling a story to Paul, who understood the language thoroughly.

CHAPTER VI.

"Y father, while yet a lad, had gained the reputation of being one of the most active *Coureurs des bois* in Upper Canada, having penetrated as far as lake Athabasca at a time when hostile tribes rendered the service one of great danger. I could tell you some of his escapes which would make your hair stand on end, and the wonder is that he never left his in the camps of the Crees, Blackfeet, or Assiniboines, by all of whom he was successively pursued, and indeed once made a prisoner, only gaining his freedom by a miracle. He had just returned from the above journey, and the prestige he had acquired was still fresh, when the news of a gigantic undertaking set on foot by Mr. John Jacob Astor, reached Montreal, and threw the whole fur-trading community into a fever of expectation."

But before returning to Pierre's story, a few words concerning this remarkable man become necessary.

The history of Mr. Astor, whose name will ever be inseparably connected with the American fur trade, is not a little curious, as demonstrating the wealth and influence which a single man may acquire by bending his whole energies to the prosecution of a single idea. Mr. Astor was a German, and at an early age quitted London, where he had resided whilst a lad, for New York, carrying with him such merchandise as he deemed suitable to the American market—chiefly musical instruments. The vessel in which he embarked was ice-bound for some months, and during his involuntary detention on board he became acquainted with a fellow passenger who exercised the trade of a furrier. This was in the year 1783, a few months after the recognition of the independence of the United States by Great Britain, and in accordance with the advice of his new friend, Astor exchanged his musical instruments in New York for furs, and hastening back to London, disposed of his stock most advantageously. From that time he turned his attention solely to peltry, studying the continental market, and making himself familiar with every branch of his new calling. Returning to New York he there took up his abode for good, making frequent journeys to Montreal and the distant trading stations in Canada. When in 1794 the obstructions which had previously existed to the export of furs were removed, Astor's intimate acquaintance with the trappers and traders of the North and West became of the greatest use, and he was soon able to send the furs he purchased to Europe and China (the best mart in the world for the furrier) in his own ships, which brought back other produce to the American market, so that he reaped a double profit, and soon became one of the wealthiest men in New York. His business extended until it embraced markets in every quarter of the globe, and it is recorded that so exact was his acquaintance with these markets, and so wide was the grasp of his mind, that he was able to guide the actions of his supercargoes and captains by the most minute instructions. At this time, while his commerce covered the seas, he was in the habit of visiting his warehouses and showing the workmen that he could equal the best of them in sorting and beating furs.

At the commencement of the present century Mr. Astor began to revolve colossal schemes for supplying all the markets in the world with furs, and for colonisation by planting towns and villages in the wilds of the western continent. He obtained the patronage of the Government for sending supply ships regularly to the Pacific coast, especially to the Russian possessions on that coast, where numerous small vessels of every nationality were in the habit of trading yearly, bartering European merchandise with the Indians for the skin of the sea-otter and other valuable furs, and shortly afterwards he attempted the great scheme of his life, which was to monopolise the fur trade from the Canadian lakes to the Pacific, by establish-- ing numerous posts, making a central depôt at the mouth of the Columbia River, and then, by obtaining one of the Sandwich Islands as a station, to supply Chinese and Indian markets with furs sent direct from the Pacific coast.

This gigantic scheme failed, as we shall see, but its grandeur was worthy the sagacity and genius of its originator.   Of course the reader must not imagine that Pierre Lefranc related the life of Mr. Astor thus at length by the side of the fire amidst Canadian snow.   The majority of what is related above was learnt by Paul subsequently, but before following the history of the expedition, I deemed it best to insert a brief sketch of its promoter, and may add that Mr. Astor's fortune was the largest ever accumulated by one man in America, amount- ing to no less a sum than four million pounds sterling, the result of good judgment, enterprise, and probity.   It is said of him, " During his whole career he hardly made a misstep through defect of his own judgment, and his memory retained for years the minutest details. He lived nearly a quarter of a century in retirement, in the society of his family, and of eminent practical and literary men, his mind retaining its vigour after his bodily strength had become enfeebled." Mr. Astor's will contained numerous charitable provisions, amongst others ten thousand pounds to the poor of Waldorf, his native village in Germany, and a splendid library to his adopted city, New York. As a child this extraordinary man had been taught to rise early, and devote a part of his first waking hours to reading the Bible, a practice that he never relinquished even when the cares of business sat most heavily upon him. He died at New York in the spring of 1848, in his seventy-fifth year. Should any of my readers feel their interest awakened, and care to pursue the subject further, I may mention that the "Life of Astor," by David Ralph Jaques, may be found in Freeman Hunt's "Lives of American Merchants," published at New York in 1858.

"Well," continued Pierre, "when the news of the formation of the 'Pacific Fur Company' reached Montreal the excitement was enormous. The North-West Company, then in the zenith of its power, was highly indignant at the audacity of the scheme, and naturally resolved to throw every stumbling block in the path of the adventurous American. But there were many retired partners and *employés* of the North-West Company who considered that they had been badly provided for, or otherwise hardly used, and the emissaries sent out by Mr. Astor found these malcontents eager to forward his views, and, from their intimate acquaintance with the Indians and the trade in general, these were the very men he wanted. Articles were signed, and the Pacific Fur Company was fairly launched, the whole of the capital being advanced by Mr. Astor, whilst the other partners contributed only their time and experience. It was decided that a depôt should be established on the Columbia River, for which purpose two parties were to set out, one by sea, the other overland; my father belonged to the former. Carried away by the prospect of wealth and steady employment he had engaged as head *voyageur*—and let me tell you that Mr. Astor was right glad to count Baptiste Lefranc amongst his followers.

"Mr. McKay, who was the leader of the sea expedition, started by water for New York in a bark-canoe, with a crew of eight Canadian *voyageurs*, of whom my father was the chief. He was quite a young man, barely two-and-twenty, and many a time has he described to me that trip down the American rivers. The Yankees rubbed their eyes with astonishment as the strange craft swept down the Hudson, the paddles flashing in the sunshine, and the echoes ringing to the *chansons* of the crew, who in their blanket capotes, striped shirts, moccassins and variegated belts, looked utter savages to the sober farmers. And when they reached New York, and paddled like lightning round the harbour, the delight of the citizens knew no bounds, and their amazement was increased when the canoe touched the shore, and the crew having jumped out, my father and another *voyageur* tossed her on to their shoulders and walked her up to Mr. Astor's house, as though she had been a feather.

"The name of the vessel that was to transport the sea party to the Columbia River was the *Tonquin*, a ship of 300 tons, mounting several guns, and commanded by Captain Thorn, a name my poor father disliked even to hear mentioned. On the 6th of September, 1810, the *Tonquin* sailed from New York, having on board fifty-five souls— twenty-two belonging to the ship, the remaining thirty-three passengers. Hardly had the vessel got into blue water before the tyrannical disposition of the captain manifested itself in his ordering all the clerks forward to mess with the seamen, a proceeding that was quite contrary to the terms of their engagement ; at the same time he treated the *voyageurs* and mechanics as though they had been dogs, abusing them as idle riff-raff, and compelling them to work night and day. It was in vain that the parties expostulated, for the captain vowed to blow out the brains of the first man who ventured to disobey his orders. Such was the commencement of the voyage, and as the time went on matters became worse and worse, until the people on board the good ship *Tonquin* were divided into two parties, and a hatred was engendered between the captain and the passengers that only terminated with the arrival of the vessel at her destination.

"At length the Falkland Islands were sighted, and the *Tonquin* came to an anchor, for the purpose of replenishing the almost exhausted water-casks. Here one of the sailors strolled away for a short time, whereupon the captain ordered the anchor to be weighed, being resolved to leave the man to his fate—starvation. With difficulty he was induced to delay his departure for an hour, during which a party went in search of the absentee. He was found enjoying a comfortable nap, the first one probably that his brutal commander had permitted him to indulge in for many a long day; but when the ship was reached the hour had been exceeded and the captain was in a fury, threatening the man's life, and maltreating those who had found him.

"At the beginning of December the *Tonquin* anchored at Egmont Bay, and both watered and refitted. Here the passengers lived ashore in a tent, and amused themselves by shooting the wild fowl with which the place abounded. And now a circumstance occurred, laughable in itself, but nearly followed by serious consequences. The water-casks were all filled up, but Captain Thorn had announced that the vessel would not move for two days, and accordingly the passengers continued in their camp. Now, one of the clerks had captured a goose, which he wished to keep alive, and so tied it to a stone about midway between the tent and the landing-place, and on the skipper landing he saw the bird, and instantly fired at it. The wretched goose flapped its wings, whereupon the captain saluted it with another charge, and running up to secure his victim, was hailed by a roar of laughter from the passengers, who had been hidden witnesses of the whole scene. In a great pet Thorn walked to his boat, and returned to the vessel, while the landsmen made merry over the skipper's blunder, and then dispersed in search of game, little suspecting the trick the angry man was playing them.

"My father was at some distance from the beach when he heard one of his companions shouting, and immediately ascending a small eminence, saw the *Tonquin* standing out to sea under full sail. The dismay and anxiety of the passengers may now be imagined, for they knew the morose temper of the captain too well to suppose that he would relent, so hurrying down to the beach where the boat lay—a little bit of a dingy, utterly unequal to carrying nine men in a seaway—they launched her, crowded in, and pulled out after the vessel. The wind was blowing very freshly, and the sea was high, so it was a mercy that she did not sink under them, more particularly as the bucket they used for a baler was dropped overboard by accident, and one of the oars broken in endeavouring to recover it. The vessel was now several miles off, and the abandoned men, among whom was the chief partner, Mr. Astor's representative, had lost all hope, when the ship was seen to wear and stand towards them. After narrowly escaping being dashed to pieces against the *Tonquin's* side, they were all got safely on board, after six hours of protracted misery in the boat, and that Captain Thorn fully intended to abandon them is evident, for he wrote from the

Sandwich Islands to Mr. Astor saying so ; and he was only prevented from carrying his purpose into effect by the determined conduct of Mr. Stuart, one of the partners, who seizing a brace of pistols threatened to shoot the unfeeling savage unless he bore up to the rescue.*

"From what I have already said you may be able to form some idea that the *Tonquin* was hardly a Paradise, and since the murderous attempt I have just related the enmity between the captain and his passengers was undisguised. Most of the latter were Scotchmen, and they talked to each other in Gaelic, whilst the Canadians spoke only in French, neither of which languages the captain could understand, and he therefore became possessed of the idea that they were plotting to displace him, and assume the command of the ship themselves, an idea which worried him half out of his life, for some of the younger men, anxious to repay him for

* It seems incredible that Captain Thorn should have confessed his deliberate intention to desert the party on shore, but in Washington Irving's "Astoria" the following extract from the original letter is given :—"Had the wind," writes Thorn to Mr. Astor, "(unfortunately) not hauled ahead soon after leaving the harbour's mouth, I should positively have left them ; and, indeed, I cannot but think it an unfortunate circumstance for you that it so happened, for the first loss in this instance would, in my opinion, have proved the best, as they seem to have no idea of the value of property, nor any apparent regard for your interest, although interwoven with their own."— " ASTORIA " (Bohn's Edition, 1850), p. 34.

his brutal treatment, often pretended to be consulting earnestly, and thus gave some colour to the
absurd suspicion. I could fill up the whole night
by telling you of the meaningless severity of this
man, but enough has been said for the present.
The *Tonquin* reached the Sandwich Islands, where
she obtained fresh provisions, and arrived off the
mouth of the Columbia River on the 22nd of
March, 1811.

"You may imagine how delighted my father and
all his fellow-sufferers were when their destination
was sighted ; for the captain had refused his per-
mission to the wish of the partners, that warm
clothing should be served out, so the poor fellows
had to shiver in their summer suits until most of
them were stricken down and confined to their
hammocks. The captain and the chief officer, Mr.
Fox, had been on bad terms for some time, owing
to the kindness for the unfortunate passengers
manifested by the latter, and the cloudy and stormy
state of the weather preventing the captain from
making out the coast, he ordered the chief mate to
examine the bar, giving him as a boat's crew, one
sailor, a very old Frenchman, and three lads wholly
unacquainted with the sea, two of them being
carters, the third a Montreal barber. Expostula-
tion with such a savage was useless, and, despite

the entreaties of the partners, the boat—a crazy, unseaworthy little nutshell—was lowered and Mr. Fox peremptorily ordered to proceed, in addition to being taunted with his justifiable hesitation. Before stepping into the boat the young man shook hands with the partners, and said, 'My uncle was drowned here not many years ago, and now I am going to lay my bones with his.' And stepping over the side he added, 'Farewell, my friends ; we will perhaps meet again in the next world.'*

"The sequel can be imagined. Mr. Fox, an excellent sailor, was utterly unacquainted with the language of the men under his command ; before the boat had proceeded a hundred yards she became unmanageable, presenting her broadside to the sea, which threatened every moment to swallow her up. Then the people in the ship, who were anxiously watching her, saw a flag held up to implore assistance. All the passengers crowded round the captain and entreated him to save the men ; his reply was an order to put the ship about, and the boat was seen no more.

"Mr. Gresham, my father was a good man, as those who knew him best can testify—a good man, a brave man, and one who would have scorned to

---

* "Adventures of the first Settlers on the Oregon or Columbia River," by Alexander Ross, one of the adventurers.—Page 55.

bear malice in his heart, yet I know this, that had
he ever met Captain Thorn on land, that ruffian's
life had not been worth a beaver-skin.   I have
heard him tell this story many hundreds of times,
and I have heard every particular confirmed by
others, yet never did he overcome the disgust and
indignation with which that man's needless barbarity inspired him.   He had seen victims slowly
done to death by the redskins, amidst horrors at
which the blood runs cold, yet to his dying day he
held the captain of the *Tonquin* as a barbarian
of infinitely blacker hue than the savage, for he
knew better.   As for me," continued honest
Pierre, " my blood boils when I think of the man
coolly letting his fellow-creatures perish.   But I
must get on with the thread of my story, unless
you are getting tired."

"Oh! no.   Pray go on," replied Paul, who had
listened with wrapt attention to this strange
narrative, and once more filling and lighting his
pipe the Canadian proceeded.

"The ship continued standing off and on until
noon of the following day, when she anchored, and
an attempt to cross the breakers was made by some
of the passengers, which nearly ended in another
catastrophe.   The bar at the mouth of the Columbia
River is a fearful one, at least three miles in length

and over this chain of sandbanks, which are continually shifting, the breakers roar with the greatest violence, covering a vast space with a sheet of white foam. The second mate was now sent to sound, and had a narrow escape of being entangled in the breakers, whereupon the third mate, named Aikens, was sent in the pinnace with the sailmaker, armourer, and two Sandwich Islanders, the mate receiving orders to hoist a flag should he find three fathoms and a half of water. This he was successful in doing, and the ship immediately weighed and stood in towards the boat, the men in the latter laying on their oars in readiness to be taken on board. What was the astonishment of every one when Captain Thorn coolly passed within twenty yards of the pinnace without offering to help them, and to the remonstrances of the partners replied, 'I can give them no assistance.' Even the second mate ventured an appeal, but the captain paid no heed, and the boat was left to its fate, the ship standing on towards the bar.

"Everything combined to endanger the vessel. The time was most badly chosen, for it was within less than an hour of sunset, and if a dangerous passage such as this must be attempted, any one with a vestige of common sense would select broad daylight; but the captain was mad or reckless, probably both, and the ship stood in, leaving the pinnace struggling with the surf. The *Tonquin* entered the breakers, rose to the swell, and then plunged headlong into the boiling waters, which decreased in depth at each moment, until at last she struck, the waves making a clear sweep of the deck, and forcing crew and passengers to seek shelter in the rigging. And then she lay battering and bumping on the bar, now whirled here, now tossed there, and utterly unmanageable. In the middle of this down came the darkness, daylight leaving them buried in the angry waves, and no great distance from the rocky coast, against which it seemed that they would inevitably be driven, if the ship hung together until they reached it. Two heavy anchors were let go, but the surf heeded them no more than if they had been boats' grapnels, and still the vessel continued to drift, seemingly to destruction. At last, when all hope had left them, the tide turned and the flood carried the battered ship into Baker's Bay, where she rested in safety, considerably more indebted to good luck than to the good management of Captain Thorn.

"On the following day that worthy, accompanied by Mr. McKay, Mr. Ross, and several others, landed, to see if they could gain any information regarding the two boats, and the party had not proceeded a hundred yards before they found the armourer standing under the shelter of a rock, and half dead from cold and misery. The poor fellow at once reproached them bitterly, and instead of replying to their inquiries concerning Mr. Aikens and his other companions, he continued murmuring, 'You did it purposely,' which undoubtedly was the truth as far as the captain was concerned. When at last he was induced to speak, he told them that after the ship had so cruelly abandoned them, the boat was drawn into the breakers, capsized, and the mate and sailmaker never rose again. The armourer and the islanders, being all expert swimmers, reached the boat, which they managed to turn on her keel, baling out some of the water, and recovering one of the oars. The tide drew the pinnace out to sea, and there they spent a miserable night from cold, exposure, and fatigue, under the effects of which the islanders lay down listlessly in the bottom of the boat, and before morning one was quite, and the other almost dead. The armourer had strength of mind enough to resist the drowsy feeling to which his companions had yielded, and occupied himself during the night in sculling the boat with their only oar. Daylight dawned, and he found that they were once more close to the breakers. Determined to effect a landing, or perish in the attempt, he turned the boat's head shorewards, and was lucky enough to have chosen a spot where she was thrown up high and dry on the beach. He had walked about a little, to restore circulation to his cramped limbs, and had then dragged the dying islander out of the boat, and covered him over with leaves for warmth; whilst thus sadly employed he had struck a path which he was following when the party met him. He and the Sandwich Islander were the only survivors of the pinnace, and as the crew of Mr. Fox's boat were never heard of again, they undoubtedly perished to a man; thus eight valuable lives were lost within sight of the future settlement by the rashness—to give it no harder name—of Captain Thorn.

"But now the vessel was safely moored in the Columbia River, and the hour to quit her hateful shelter had arrived—an hour welcomed by my father and by every one of the *Tonquin's* passengers. They had been treated like dogs on board, so it was no wonder they felt glad to get away. But it is getting late, Monsieur Paul, and as Monsieur Groves shows no sign of turning up, we will go to sleep now, and I can finish my father's experiences in Oregon to-morrow night. *Ah! mes amis*, I shall have some of your feet in my trap soon," he added, shaking his fist at the wolves, which were howling around the carcase of the moose, and relapsing into his broken English once more as he finished his narrative.

Tired out by the varied incidents of the day, Paul raised no objections to the Canadian's proposal, and wrapping themselves in their buffalo robes, with their feet in almost dangerous proximity to the fire, the hunters were soon both buried in sleep.

CHAPTER VII.

AT early dawn both Pierre and Gresham were astir. After breakfast the
Canadian looked to his traps, saw
that the springs were in good order
and worked freely, after which they
sallied forth to set them, an operation that
Paul looked forward to with great curiosity;
for he was determined to become master of
all branches of the fur trade, and it is needless to
say that trapping stands first in importance. And
now came into use the hand-sledge that Pierre
had brought with him, formed of a thin piece of
board six feet in length, turned up at the end, and
having a network at either side to prevent the
loading from slipping off. Upon this the Canadian
piled his traps, an axe, some moose flesh for bait,
and slinging his gun by the strap over his shoulder
the hunter marched off, dragging the little sleigh
after him by a cord of sufficient length to prevent
its over-riding his snow-shoes. Paul walked by his
side, and they soon reached the place where the

moose lay, that is to say its skeleton, for the wolves had been hard at work all night, and had stripped every ounce of flesh off the huge carcase. All round were the marks of their feet, and Pierre chuckled as he set his traps baited with a piece of singed moose flesh, and concealed them carefully in the snow. The instruments used to capture the wolf are powerful steel gins exactly resembling those set by poachers and rat-catchers in England, with the exception that they are toothless, and have two springs in place of one. Wolves are so cunning that the hunter generally lays two traps side by side, one baited, the other entirely concealed in the snow, so that whilst the wary animal is trying to dislodge the tempting morsel without injury to himself, he frequently steps upon the hidden danger and finds himself caught by the leg. These traps are each provided with an iron chain, to which the trapper fastens a stout stick, and when the captive drags the trap the stick hitches in the undergrowth, and so far impedes his progress that the hunter has little difficulty in tracking and killing him. If the traps were fastened down, some of the animals, in their anxiety to escape, would gnaw off their own legs, and many instances are recorded of three-legged foxes being seen at large, who had undoubtedly sacrificed a limb to gain their liberty.

The fox and wolf traps are exactly alike in every particular except size, and the method of setting one applies perfectly to the other; the springs are so powerful *that it requires a man's whole strength to open them.* When set, the jaws of the trap are exactly on a level with the snow, under which both chain and stick are perfectly concealed, and the bait is scattered around. No mark is made by the trapper to denote the presence of his snares, and one of the chief difficulties under which the novice labours is to find their whereabouts in the pathless forest.

Of wolves there are several kinds in America, the black, grey, red, and Arctic. Except in their colour these all resemble each other very closely, and are seldom dangerous to man unless driven by hunger. One instance, however, is mentioned in which the black wolf showed determined ferocity. Two young negroes, who resided near the banks of the Ohio River, in Kentucky, had sweethearts living on another plantation about four miles distant, and after their work was over for the day the young men were in the habit of visiting the ladies of their love ; the nearest way to whose dwelling lay across a large cane brake, and as to the lovers every moment was of consequence, they usually took this lonely route to save time. Winter had set in cold,

dark, and dreary, and after sunset scarcely a glimpse
of light or glow of warmth was to be found save in
the bosoms of the young lovers who boldly penetrated these gloomy solitudes. One night they set
forth undeterred by the snow, a thin coating of
which covered the ground, and rendered the little
frequented path almost undistinguishable. As
though foreboding evil they took the precaution to
carry their axes, in the use of which the plantation
negroes are remarkably expert, and hurried forward
as rapidly as the tangled track would allow. The
darkness was intense, though now and then a break
in the trees slightly lessened the gloom, or a leaden
cloud rifting asunder allowed them a transient
glimpse of a feeble star. As they pushed on
silently, but resolutely, a fearful howl arose which
froze the very blood in their veins, for they knew
too well the cry of the hungry wolf, and rightly
judged that they were surrounded by a pack of
these famished demons. Instinctively they paused
for a few moments, during which the beating of
their hearts was almost audible—the darkness
showed them nothing—and an ominous silence
reigned around. Whispering comfort and hope to
each other, and holding their axes in readiness,
the lovers again stepped forward, but before a dozen
yards were covered the foremost was assailed by

several ferocious enemies, who inflicted terrible wounds with their fangs on his legs and arms, and despite his struggles brought him to the ground. Both the young men fought manfully. With sweeping blows the one who still kept his feet strove to free his companion, but in his own flesh the cruel teeth sheathed themselves, and hastily passing his hand over his prostrate companion he knew him to be past mortal aid. Self-preservation only was to be thought of, so hurling his axe at the almost invisible foes, the survivor grasped the bough of a friendly tree, and had just sufficient strength to draw himself up into a place of safety. Here he passed the night—a night of horror, for his wounds became stiff and painful; and under his feet he could hear the savage fiends riving and tearing, he had little difficulty in guessing at *what.* Morning came at length, and he beheld the bones of his friend, beside which three gaunt black wolves were lying dead, while the snow around was stained with his heart's blood. The rest of the pack had disappeared, so quitting his shelter and recovering his axe the horrified young man crawled slowly home to relate the fearful catastrophe.

The general appearance of the wolf is so well known that it needs no description; and furious as the animal undoubtedly is when driven by hunger, when trapped, and escape is hopeless, it becomes the most abject and ignoble coward. To illustrate this I quote the following from M. Audubon. "After putting up our horses and refreshing ourselves, we entered into conversation with our worthy host (a farmer) and were invited by him to visit the wolf pits which he had constructed about half a mile from the house. Glad of the opportunity, we accompanied him across the fields to the skirts of the adjoining forest, where he had three pits within a few hundred yards of each other. They were about eight feet deep, broadest at the bottom, so as to render it impossible for the most active animal to escape from them. The mouth of each pit was covered with a revolving platform of boughs and twigs, interlaced together and attached to a cross piece of timber, which served for an axle. On this light sort of platform, which was balanced by a heavy stick of wood fastened to the under side, a large piece of putrid venison was tied for bait. After examining all the pits, we returned to the house, our companion remarking that he was in the habit of visiting his pits daily, in order to see that all was right ; that the wolves had been very bad that season ; had destroyed nearly all his sheep, and had killed one of his colts. 'But,' added he, 'I am now paying them off in full, and if I have any luck, you will see some fun in the morning.' With this expectation we retired to rest, and were up at daylight. 'I think,' said our host, 'that all is right ; for I see the dogs are anxious to get away to the pits, and although they are nothing but curs, their noses are pretty keen for wolves.' As he took up his gun, and axe, and a large knife, the dogs began to howl and bark, and whisked round us, as if full of delight. When we reached the first pit, we found the bait had been disturbed and the platform was somewhat injured, but the animal was not in the pit ; on examining the second pit, we discovered three famous fellows safe enough in it, two black and one brindled, all of good size. They were lying flat on the earth, with their ears close down to their heads, their eyes indicating fear more than anger. To our astonishment, the farmer proposed descending into the pit to hamstring them, in order to haul them up, and then allow them to be killed by the dogs, which, he said, would sharpen his curs for an encounter with the wolves, should any come near his house in future. Being novices in this kind of business, we begged to be lookers-on. 'With all my heart,' cried the farmer, 'stand here, and look at me,' whereupon he glided down, on a knotted pole, taking his axe and knife with him, and leaving his rifle to our care. We were not a little surprised at the cowardice of the wolves. The woodman stretched out their hind legs, in succession, and with a stroke of the knife cut the principal tendon above the joint, exhibiting as little fear as if he had been marking lambs. As soon as he had thus disabled the wolves, he got out, but had to return to the house for a rope, which he had not thought of. He returned quickly, and, whilst I secured the platform in a perpendicular position on its axis, he make a slip-knot at one end of the rope, and threw it over the head of one of the wolves. We now hauled the terrified animal up ; and motionless with fright, half choked, and disabled in its hind legs, the farmer slipped the rope from its neck and left it to the mercy of the dogs, who set upon it with great fury, and worried it to death. The second was dealt with in the same manner ; but the third, which was probably oldest, showed some spirit the moment the dogs were set upon it, and scuffled along on its forelegs at a surprising rate, snapping all the while furiously at the dogs, several of which it bit severely; and so well did the desperate animal defend itself, that the farmer, apprehensive of its killing some of his pack, ran up and knocked it on the head with his axe. This wolf was a female, and was blacker than the other dark-coloured one."

All the wolf tribe are in the habit of feigning
death when they find that escape is impossible, and
will often deceive even an experienced hunter.
Their tenacity of life is most extraordinary, and a
wolf that had been belaboured until it was thought
that every bone in its body was broken, has got up,
shaken itself, and slunk away apparently little the
worse.   There is a smaller species of this animal
inhabiting the open country in America, and known
as the Prairie wolf, but into its habits I shall not
enter here.

We now come to the foxes, of which there are
several kinds, all of which are eagerly sought after
by the fur hunter.   The most beautiful of these is
the black or silver fox, whose skin stands second
only to the sea-otter in value, fetching from twenty-
five to forty guineas in the London market, whilst
a well-matched pair are more valuable still.   A fox
may be said to be a fox all the world over, therefore I need say nothing of its shape, with which
everyone is familiar, but pass on to its valuable fur.
The body of the silver fox is clothed with two kinds
of hair, an outer and an inner coat.   The longer or
outer hair extends two inches beyond the shorter
or under fur, especially on the neck, beneath the
throat, behind the shoulders, along the flanks, and
on the tail ; this hair is soft, glossy, and finer than

that of the sable. The under fur is unusually long and dense, measuring in some places two inches, and is exceedingly fine, feeling to the hand as soft as the finest cotton wool and surrounding the whole body even to the tail ; the hair composing this fur, when viewed separately, exhibits a crimped or wavy appearance, and so thoroughly has nature armed this animal against the severe climate it frequents, that the very soles of the feet are thickly clothed with woolly hair, leaving no callous spots visible. From its great length and density the beauty of this fur may be imagined, and its colouring considerably enhances its appearance. The under fur is uniformly of a chocolate brown, whilst the hairs on the neck, and on a dorsal line extending to the root of the tail, are black. Some skins are perfectly black, others of a bluish-gray, but it is most commonly found with parts of its fur hoary, the shiny black coat being thickly interspersed with white tipped hairs, from which circumstance it derives its name of the "silver" fox. The tail is tipped with white, by which it can always be recognised, though there is little chance of mistaking so beautiful an animal. Like all of its tribe, the silver fox is very shy, and the trappers have marvellous tales of its cunning and sagacity. Its scientific name is *canis argentatus.*

The other species of fox, the red, the arctic, and

the cross require no other description than their name conveys. The latter derives his name from a cruciform mark running down the back and over the shoulders, and not from any infirmity of temper.

The steel traps having been set wherever the Canadian thought there was most chance of success, the companions proceeded in search of the sign of pine martens, fishers, and other fur-bearing animals of the weazel tribe. Two diminutive tracks were at length found, which the trapper pronounced to be martens, and at once set to work constructing a fall trap for their capture. Mr. Lord describes this operation as follows: "To commence, we must build a half-circle, with large stones, to the height of about three feet; this done, we next procure a tolerably heavy tree, drag it to the stone building we have constructed, and lay it across the entrance. The heavy end should be the furthest away, the lighter end we poise carefully upon an arrangement of peeled sticks. As a familiar example of what I mean, I may instance the figure-of-four trap used by boys for catching small birds. This contrivance and one end of the tree or 'fall' are together supported on a smooth stick, which is built in amongst the stones composing the half-circle. This support stick must project horizontally from the centre of the hollow of the wall, at a height of about three feet from the ground; it needs to be firmly fixed, and must be tapered to a point, and polished as smooth as an ebony ruler. The length of this support has to be regulated by the depth of the side walls; its pointed end ought to be just six inches within the entrance walls, against the ends of which the tree or 'fall' traverses. A tempting bit of rabbit or grouse, carefully skinned, for the marten is most fastidious in its tastes—if the meat is at all tainted or dirtied in the preparation it is useless as a lure—is securely fastened to a loop of cord made from the inner bark of the cedar tree (*Thuja gigantea*); this loop is slid upon the supporting stick, and pushed on until it reaches the hindermost part of the wall. Now, we make the figure of four, which rests upon the horizontal bar, and at the same time bearsup the tree or 'fall.' The figure of four is easily made; the vertical piece has two notches cut in it, one in the centre for the horizontal piece to rest and fit in, and a second in the top to receive the end of the oblique piece, which is cut to a wedge-shape at both ends. The horizontal piece has one notch to take the end of the oblique; on the other rests the fall. We have set our trap, and now, as a final process, we walk backwards from it for some distance, and carefully brush away every trace of our foot-prints with a pine branch; and here

K

for the time we must leave it. We shall see how it acts when we again visit the trap.

" The 'fall' is down, and underneath it, crushed and lifeless, is stretched a fine male marten. If you observe the position the body lies in, it will explain to some extent the care that was needed in rightly adjusting the length of the support in reference to the 'fall.' The tree has dropped upon the marten immediately behind the shoulders, and so caused instant death ; and here let me explain how the trap acts. The marten, hunting about, suddenly sniffs the dainty bait suspended from the horizontal stick ; approaching the trap, and having satisfied its naturally suspicious nature that there is nothing very formidable in a pile of sticks and stones —and from our precaution of brushing out the foot-prints, it is unable to scent the presence of an enemy—ventures to creep under the 'fall,' and enter the semi-circle of stones; then reaching up, the marten seizes the bait, and struggles with all the strength it can exert to pull it down ; but finding this is not to be accomplished, next tries what backing out and tugging the coveted morsel after it will do. The stick, if you remember, was made as smooth as an ebony ruler, and so the animal finds the bait and loop easily traverses it towards the entrance of the trap ; but when half the marten's body is without the 'fall,' the loop comes against the verticle stick composing the figure of four, which rests upon the stick along which the victim is impatiently dragging the loop to which the bait is fast. Finding this unlooked-for obstruction makes him irritable, and so he concentrates all his energies for a sudden jerk. 'Tis done, the support of the 'fall' tumbles in pieces to the ground, and the heavy tree slips down suddenly upon the marten's back. You will thus observe, that the grand secret in setting a 'fall' trap of this pattern is so to adjust the figure of four upon the stick from which the bait is suspended, that when the final tug is made, nearly two-thirds of the marten's body shall be outside and clear of the tree placed for the purpose of crushing his life out."

Though the description of this trap occupies a good deal of space, yet an expert trapper can construct nearly half a hundred a-day, but the polished sticks must be provided beforehand. Where stones are not handy for building the semi-oval enclosure, stakes driven into the ground will answer the purpose. Until night-fall the Canadian and Paul busied themselves in the construction of these traps, and then returned to their camp pretty well tired out. They found no signs of Groves, but Pierre said that most likely the chase had carried him a long distance, and the time for the rendezvous was hardly yet expired.

But though I have entered at length upon the kind of trap in which the marten is captured, I have said very little about the animal itself, and as it forms one of the principal items in the fur trade some slight account of its appearance and habits will be in place here.

The generic name of all the animals of this tribe, namely the fisher, marten, mink, ermine, &c., is *Mustela* or Weasel. Let us commence with the fisher.

This animal is known as Pennant's Marten by naturalists, and by trappers as the Black Cat or Fisher. Its scientific name is *Mustela Canadensis.* The head of the fisher somewhat resembles that of a dog, and its body is long and admirably formed for both agility and strength. The legs are short, with strong, sharp, curved nails, and the toes on all the feet are connected at the base by a short hairy web, so that the callosities only make a slight impression when the animal is walking or running on the snow. The tail is long, bushy, and gradually diminishing to a point towards the extremity. The fisher possesses a strong smell of musk. The general colour is a most beautiful chestnut brown, in some specimens approaching to black. Its length, exclusive of the tail, is about two feet, and its weight perhaps ten pounds. The fisher climbs trees with the greatest facility, in fact it is amongst their branches that it usually seeks its prey. Though living in the woods, it prefers damp places in the vicinity of water, and is said by one naturalist to prey upon frogs in the summer season, though its favourite food is the Canadian porcupine, which it kills by biting the under portion of the animal's body, where there are no quills. The fisher makes its nest in hollow trees, or rather it takes possession of the ready-made home of the squirrel, and to avoid any disputes with the rightful owner, kills and eats him, off-hand. It is said to throw itself down from lofty boughs, and to fall on the ground without injury, but there is reason to doubt the accuracy of this statement. A party had once ascended a mountain in search of rare plants, and being fatigued had seated themselves on a rock, when a grey squirrel was observed to dart past at full speed and in a great fright, closely pursued by a fisher. Both animals were too much occupied with their own concerns to notice the on-lookers, who thus obtained an excellent view of the whole affair. Fast as the squirrel ran the fisher was rapidly overhauling it, when the former sought refuge in the boughs of a cucumber tree, still pursued by its hungry foe. The squirrel leaped lightly among the smaller branches on which the heavier animal seemed disinclined to trust its weight, but in its fright it miscalculated a distance, and fell from one of the topmost boughs, lighting unhurt upon the rocks beneath. Now was the time for the fisher to have exhibited his tumbling propensities had he possessed them, but instead of leaping boldly after his prey he commenced running down the stem of the tree. At this point the bystanders interfered, and advanced to the foot of the tree which the fisher was descending. He paused on the opposite side, as if trying to ascertain whether he had been observed, and no one of the party carrying a gun they commenced hammering on their tin botanizing boxes with the handles of their knives, a measure which filled the fisher with consternation, and the greater the noise became the more his terror increased, and in terrible trepidation he re-ascended the tree, sprang to another, down whose stem he ran until within twenty feet of the bottom, when he made a flying leap to the ground and in a few moments was out of sight. The title "fisher" is evidently a misnomer, for the animal is not amphibious in its habits; the Canadian hunters always call it the Pekan.

The next animal of the tribe possessing valuable

fur is the pine-marten (*Mustela Martes*), which is found in all the forests of North America, but, unlike the fisher, it frequents the driest parts. In form the marten resembles an English ferret. Its fur is about an inch and a quarter long, of a pale, dull, greyish-brown from the roots upwards, dull, brownish-yellow near the summit, and tipped with dark brown or black; the lustre of the surface of the fur is considerable, and it is often palmed off on purchasers as a more costly kind, for which purpose it is dyed any desired colour. The marten is from eighteen to twenty-two inches in length, exclusive of the tail, and its weight about six pounds.

Audubon says, "Let us take a share of the cunning and sneaking character of the fox, as much of the wide-awake and cautious habits of the weasel, a similar proportion of the voracity (and a little of the fetid odour) of the mink, and add thereto some of the climbing propensities of the racoon, and we have a tolerable idea of the attributes of the pine-marten." As may easily be imagined from the above this little beast is shy, cruel, cunning and active ; but differs from the animals to which it has been likened in never approaching the residence of man, but rather keeping to the dense forests, where it can prey upon birds, their eggs and young, squirrels, mice, shrews, wood-rats, &c., together with beetles, toads, and lizards. It is also an eater of certain nuts and berries, and resembles the bear in a fondness for honey. It derives its name from the pine forests in the northern part of America, to which it shows a decided preference, but is known amongst furriers as the American Sable. The darker the skins the more valuable they become, and the rocky and mountainous but woody district of the Nipigon, on the north side of Lake Superior, has long been noted for its black and valuable marten-skins. Though it does not frequent human habitations, the marten finds out the hoards of meat and fish laid up by the natives, and if they have inadvertently left a crevice open, it squeezes its lithe body through, and destroys right and left. When its retreat is cut off, this little animal displays the greatest courage, showing its keen teeth, setting up its hair, arching its back, and making a hissing noise, like a cat. If attacked by a dog it will fearlessly seize the aggressor by its nose, and gives him so shrewd a nip, that unless trained to the combat, it is usually very glad to let its would-be captive escape. It is easily tamed, when it loses much of its snappish disposition, and manifests an attachment for its master. The Indians frequently eat its flesh, but to European tastes it is rank, coarse, and pervaded with the musky odour peculiar to all this tribe. The female is smaller than the male, and is very prolific, bringing forth five and six young ones at a birth. That they were very plentiful formerly may be gathered from Sir John Richardson, who records that upwards of a hundred thousand skins were collected annually in the fur countries.

We next come to the mink or minx otter *(Putorius Vison)* which is the only animal of the genus *mustela* inhabiting the northern parts of America that can be said to live in the water, and the name of "fisher" could with much justice be transferred from its present bearer to the mink. It has a long, slender body, with a small depressed head, short flat nose, small eyes which are placed far forward, broad rounded ears covered with hair, very long neck, and short stout legs. The feet and palms are covered with hair even to the extremity of the nails; and the tail, which is round and thick at the roots, tapering towards the end, is covered with long horizontal hairs, which give it a bushy appearance ; there are two brown-coloured glands situated on each side of the under surface of the tail, which have a small cavity lined by a thin, white-wrinkled membrane, and these cells contain a strong musky fluid, the smell of which is rather disagreeable. The coat is composed of two kinds of hair, upper and under. The latter is soft and downy, and the long upper hair entirely conceals it. The colour of the mink is usually a rich chocolate brown, with a white patch under the throat and on the breast. Its length from the nose to the root of the tail is about fifteen inches, and the tail from seven to eight. There is nothing very remarkable about its habits, except that it commits fearful ravages amongst poultry. Sir John Richardson says: " The vison passes much of its time in the water, and when pursued seeks shelter in that element in preference to endeavouring to escape by land, on which it travels slowly. It swims and dives well, and can remain a considerable time under water. Its short fur, forming a smooth glossy coat, its tail exactly like that of an otter, and the shortness of its legs, denote its aquatic habits. It preys upon small fish, fish-spawn, fresh-water mussels, &c., in the summer; but in the winter, when its watery haunts are frozen over, it will hunt mice on land, or travel to a considerable distance through the snow in search of a rapid or fall, where there is still some open water. The vison, when irritated, exhales, next to the skunk, the most fetid odour of any animal in the fur countries. It is not very timid when in the water, and will approach near to a canoe out of curiosity, diving, however, instantly on perceiving the flash of a gun, or any movement

from whence it apprehends danger. It is easily
tamed, and is capable of strong attachment. In a
domestic state it is observed to sleep much in the
day, and to be fond of warmth. One, which I saw
in the possession of a Canadian woman, passed
the day in her pocket, looking out occasionally
when its attention was roused by any unusual
noise."

Audubon also bears testimony to the gentle disposition of the mink. He says, "We had in our
possession a pet of this kind for eighteen months ;
it regularly made a visit to an adjoining fish-pond
both morning and evening, and returned to the
house of its own accord, where it continued during
the remainder of the day. It waged war against
the Norway rats which had their domicile in the
dam that formed the fish-pond, and it caught the
frogs which had taken possession of its banks. We
did not perceive that it captured many fish, and it
never attacked the poultry. It was on good terms
with the dogs and cats, and molested no one unless
its tail or foot was accidentally trod upon, when it
invariably revenged itself by snapping at the foot of
the offender. It was rather dull at mid-day, but
very active and playful in the morning and evening
and at night. It never emitted its disagreeable
odour except when it had received a sudden and

severe hurt. It was fond of squatting in the chimney-corner, and formed a particular attachment to an arm-chair in our study."

Such is a brief account of the principal fur-bearing animals of the genus *mustela*, but the list would be sadly incomplete were I to leave out a little creature whose fur is the emblem of high rank— the ermine.

The ermine (*Mustela Erminea*) is nothing more than the common stoat with which the reader is probably familiar. It doubtless seems odd that the robes of our peers and other dignitaries should be trimmed with the skins of vermin, but such nevertheless is the fact. The ermine has a convex nose and forehead, a long slender body, long cylindrical tail, and short limbs. In the winter time the fur of some specimens is of a pure white colour throughout, except on the end of the tail, which, together with a few anterior whiskers, are black. In other specimens there is a bright primrose-yellow tinge on the belly, the posterior part of the back, or the tail. The feet in the winter are clothed with hair on the soles, which project so as to conceal the claws. In the summer the soles are nearly naked, and the fur on the upper parts resembles that of the common weasel in colour. The length of the ermine is about ten inches, exclusive of the tail, which measures perhaps five inches, of which about three are black both in summer and winter.

The change of colour in these little animals is very curious. Messrs. Audubon and Bachman say, "As far as our observations have enabled us to form an opinion on this subject, we have arrived at the conclusion that the animal sheds its coat twice a year, *i.e.*, at the periods when these semi-annual changes take place. In autumn, the summer hair gradually and almost imperceptibly drops out, and is succeeded by a fresh coat of hair, which in the course of two or three weeks becomes pure white ; while in the spring the animal undergoes its change from white to brown in consequence of shedding its winter coat, the new hairs then coming out brown. We have in our possession a specimen captured in November, in which the change of colour has considerably advanced, but is not completed. The whole of the under surface, the sides, neck, and body to within half an inch of the back, together with the legs, are white, as well as the edges of the ears. On the upper surface, the nose, forehead, neck, and an irregular line on the back, together with a spot on the outer surface of the fore-leg, are brown, showing that these parts change colour last."

Beautiful as the ermine is in the purity of its spotless white, a more mischievous little animal amongst poultry can hardly be imagined, for it is animated by an intuitive blood-thirstiness and love of destruction which prompts it to slaughter every animal or bird within its reach, some of which are ten times its own size, as the hare or domestic fowl. The gentlemen quoted above proceed to say, "It is a noted and hated depredator of the poultry-house, and we have known forty well-grown fowls to have been killed in one night by a single ermine. Satiated with the blood of probably a single fowl, the rest, like the flock slaughtered by the wolf in the sheepfold, were destroyed in obedience to a law of nature, an instinctive propensity to kill. We have traced the footsteps of this blood-sucking little animal on the snow, pursuing the trail of the American rabbit, and although it could not overtake its prey by superior speed, yet the timid hare soon sought refuge in the hollow of a tree, or in a hole dug by the marmot or skunk. Thither it was pursued by the ermine, and destroyed, the skin and other remains at the mouth of the burrow bearing evidence of the fact. We observed an ermine, after having captured a hare of the above species, first behead it and then drag the body some twenty yards over the fresh-fallen snow, beneath which it was concealed, and the snow tightly pressed over it, the little prowler displaying thereby a habit of which we became aware for the first time on that occasion. To avoid a dog that was in close pursuit, it mounted a tree and laid itself flat on a limb about twenty feet from the ground, from which it was finally shot. We have ascertained by successful experiments, repeated more than a hundred times, that the ermine can be employed, in the manner of the ferret of Europe, in driving our American rabbit from the burrow into which it has retreated. In one instance, the ermine employed had been captured only a few days before, and its canine teeth were filed in order to prevent its destroying the rabbit ; a cord was placed around its neck to secure its return. It pursued the hare through all the windings of its burrow and forced it to the mouth, where it could be taken in a net, or by the hand. In winter, after a snow storm, the ruffled grouse has a habit of plunging into the loose snow, where it remains at times for one or two days. In this passive state the ermine sometimes detects and destroys it. In an unsuccessful attempt at domesticating this grouse by fastening its feet to a board in the mode adopted with the stool pigeon, and placing it high on a shelf, an ermine, which we had kept as a pet, found its way by the curtains of the window, and put an end to our experiment by eating off the head of our grouse.

" Notwithstanding all these mischievous and destructive habits, it is doubtful whether the ermine
is not rather a benefactor than an enemy to the
farmer, ridding his granaries and fields of many
depredators on the product of his labour, that
would devour ten times the value of the poultry
and eggs which, at long and uncertain intervals, it
occasionally destroys. A mission appears to have
been assigned it by Providence to lessen the rapidly
multiplying number of mice of various species, and
the smaller rodentia.

" Wherever an ermine has taken up its residence,
the mice in its vicinity for half a mile round have
been found rapidly to diminish in number. Their
active little enemy is able to force its thin
vermiform body into the burrows, it follows them
to the end of their galleries, and destroys whole
families. We have on several occasions, after a
light snow, followed the trail of this weasel through
fields and meadows, and witnessed the immense
destruction which it occasioned in a single night.
It enters every hole under logs, stumps, stone-heaps
and fences, and evidences of its bloody deeds are
seen in the mutilated remains of the mice scattered
on the snow. The little chipping or ground squirrel,
Tamias Lysteri, takes up its residence in the vicinity
of the grain fields, and is known to carry off in its

cheek-pouches vast quantities of wheat and buck-wheat, to serve as winter stores. The ermine in-stinctively discovers these snug retreats, and in the space of a few minutes destroys a whole family of these beautiful little *tamiæ;* without even resting awhile until it has consumed its now abundant food, its appetite craving for more blood, as if impelled by an irresistible destiny, it proceeds in search of other objects on which it may glut its insatiable vampire-like thirst. The Norway rat and the common house-mouse take possession of our barns, wheat stacks and granaries, and destroy vast quantities of grain. In some instances the farmer is reluctantly compelled to pay even more than a tithe in contributions towards the support of these pests. Let, however, an ermine find its way into these barns and granaries, and there take up its winter residence, and the havoc which is made among the rats and mice will soon be observable. The ermine pursues them to their farthest retreats, and in a few weeks the premises are entirely free from their depredations. We once placed a half-domesticated ermine in an outhouse infested with rats, shutting up the holes on the outside to prevent their escape. The little animal soon commenced his work of destruction. The squeaking of the rats was heard throughout the day. In the evening it

L

came out licking its mouth, and seeming like a hound after a long chase, much fatigued. A board of the floor was raised to enable us to ascertain the result of our experiment, and an immense number of rats were observed, which, although they had been killed on different parts of the building, had been dragged together, forming a compact heap."

I shall wind up this long chapter with the following curious story of ermines or stoats, related by Mr. Wood in the first volume of his " Illustrated Natural History."

"A gentleman was walking along a road near Cricklade, when he saw two stoats sitting in the path. He idly picked up a stone, and flung it at the animals, one of which was struck, and was knocked over by the force of the blow. The other stoat immediately uttered a loud and peculiar cry, which was answered by a number of its companions, who issued from a neighbouring hedge, and sprang upon their assailant, running up his body with surprising rapidity, and striving to reach his neck. As soon as he saw the stoats coming to the attack, he picked up a handful of stones, thinking that he should be able to repel his little enemies, but they came boldly on, in spite of the stones and of his stick. Most providentially, a sharp wind happened to be blowing on that day, and he had wound a thick woollen comforter round his neck, so that he was partially protected. Finding that he had no chance of beating off the pertinacious animals, he flung his stick down, fixed his hat firmly over his temples, and pressing his hands to his neck, so as to guard that perilous spot as much as possible from the sharp teeth of the stoats, set off homewards as fast as he could run. By degrees, several of the animals dropped off, but others clung so determinately to their opponent, that when he arrived at his stables no less than five stoats were killed by his servants as they hung on his person. His hands, face, and part of his neck were covered with wounds; but, owing to the presence of mind with which he had defended his neck, the large blood-vessels had escaped without injury. The distance from the spot where he had been attacked to his own house was nearly four miles. He always declared that when he struck the stoat with the stone, its companion called out 'Murder.'"

The ermine is very prolific, bringing forth from five to twelve young ones at a birth. These are born about April or May, and are of a pale yellow colour. It avoids water, and if forcibly thrown into it, swims awkwardly, like a cat, and, unlike the fisher and pine marten, it never pursues its prey on trees; in fact it rarely leaves the ground, except to escape from its two worst enemies, men and dogs. The ermine is easily caught in almost any kind of trap, for though cautious it is both bold and inquisitive, and at one time ermine-skins formed part of the *menues pelletries* exported from Canada ; but their value at present is so little, that they do not repay the Hudson's Bay Company the expense of collecting ; hence very few are brought to England from that quarter.

After supper was finished and the pipes lit, Paul requested the Canadian to continue his story, which he did as follows.

165

CHAPTER VIII.

"I THINK, Monsieur Paul, that I left off last night having brought the *Tonquin* safely to an anchor in the Columbia River. Well, for some days the adventurers looked about for a suitable spot on which to build the depôt, and finally selected a rising piece of ground distant about twelve miles from the bar that had proved fatal to eight of their number. On the 12th of April, 1811, the whole party joyfully quitted the ship and the iron rule of Captain Thorn, to encamp on shore. I say joyfully only insomuch as it applies to escaping from the tyranny of the captain, for the recent disasters had cast a gloom over all, and even my father's light heart was oppressed by melancholy forebodings, which the character of the surrounding country was little calculated to allay. In front lay the inlet with its frowning and rocky shores, whilst the ever-foaming breakers on the distant bar were clearly visible to the west. On the other hand the landscape was wild and rugged, and looking south an endless forest of giant trees extended as far as the eye could reach. To establish a camp, many of these forest kings had to be felled, and when I mention that some of them were full fifty feet in girth, standing close together amidst huge boulders of rock, the difficulties before the settlers may be imagined. The command was assumed by Mr. Duncan McDougall, whose temper unfortunately was none of the best, and under his direction every man set to work clearing away the undergrowth, their guns standing within arm's length, for at any moment they were liable to an attack from the hostile Indians prowling in the dense covert that surrounded them.

"On their first arrival the natives had shown themselves friendly, and under the direction of their chief, Comecomly, had assisted in saving the crew of the long boat when she was swamped, but their attitude now indicated a disposition to treachery, and the settlers were compelled to hold themselves in readiness to meet any attack. My father was a good axeman, and he used always to smile when relating the efforts made by the adventurers to fell the forest trees. Being all *voyageurs*, traders, or Sandwich Islanders, few of them had ever handled an axe before or for that matter even a gun, and their attempts to cope with the giant pines were most ludicrous. Every man, without exception, from the highest to the lowest, had to take his share in the arduous work, and this was their method of proceeding. Four people were told off to each tree, around which they erected a sort of scaffolding, from which they commenced their attack. The axes were of all shapes and sizes ; and in hands unaccustomed to their use, but little headway was made ; the tree was notched and hacked about in every direction, but that was all. At last some one announced that it was on the point of falling, upon which there was a speedy retreat from the scaffolding, and all hands stood wondering which direction it would take, for they had no idea of 'laying' it. Several minutes would pass, but the giant showed no sign of yielding, standing stubbornly upright and seeming to defy their utmost efforts. At last some one more adventurous than the rest, would remount the scaffold and hew away afresh ; showers of splinters would fly ; a creaking noise arose, and with a groan the pine tree bowed his lofty head, but not to reach the ground, for it invariably caught in the boughs of a neighbour, and there hung a constant menace to the whole party. As my father said, it was heart-breaking work and at the end of two months hardly an acre had been cleared, whilst three men had been killed by the natives, two wounded by falling timber, and another had blown off his hand whilst blasting a stump, in addition to which calamities the whole party were worn out by fatigue and night-watching.

"But you must not imagine, Monsieur Paul, that because the adventurers had left the *Tonquin* they were quit of her estimable captain. That worthy had received orders to coast along towards the north and trade with the Indians, after he had disembarked his passengers ; and he was now seized with an intense anxiety to depart, and became furious because store-houses were not erected for the reception of the goods. Petty trade was also carried on with Comecomly and his tribe, which raised the captain's spleen, who complained bitterly of his ship being turned upside down for the sake of a few ragamuffin Indians. Angry letters passed between McDougall and himself, but at last buildings were run up, the goods and the frame of a coasting vessel that was to be fitted together for river service were landed at Astoria, for by that name was the new settlement christened, and the *Tonquin* was at liberty to depart whenever her commander saw fit.

"This expedition seemed from the outset to be

destined to misfortune. I mentioned that Mr. McDougall was a man of bad temper, and he succeeded in making himself so unpopular that one fine morning four men were found missing; they were, however, seized by the Indians when they had gone eighty miles up the river, and delivered up on payment of a heavy ransom. Their desertion was so far productive of good that it opened the leader's eyes to the discontent which prevailed around him; and when six more men ran away— to be returned in the same manner—he changed for the better, serving out tents for the sick, and allowing them little delicacies which he had hitherto reserved for himself. That Mr. Astor showed little of his usual foresight in not sending a medical man with the expedition is now universally acknowledged.

"But internal feuds were not all the party had to contend against. Comecomly and his followers spread a report that the neighbouring tribes were uniting for the purpose of destroying the adventurers, and a foreboding of approaching danger was added to their other troubles. To convince the natives that no harm was designed them several parties were sent into the interior, and my father accompanied Mr. McKay in a canoe up the river until they reached the Cascades, a distance of nearly two hundred miles from Astoria. The trip lasted twelve days, and they returned well satisfied with both the natives and the country.

" Mr. McKay had been in the North West Company, where he had gained a reputation for activity and eccentricity. That he carried the latter quality to a somewhat dangerous length the following anecdote of my father's will prove. It is customary on great trading occasions to select a tall tree, from which the boughs are all lopped, which, having the trader's name cut on the trunk, may stand as a memorial of his visit. On McKay's return from the Cascades he resolved on making such a trophy, and directed one of his men to climb a tree and prepare it. In the hope of getting a glass of grog as a reward, the man obeyed the order with alacrity; but no sooner had he ascended to the summit than the facetious trader lighted a fire at the bottom, and the whole tree was soon in a blaze. The wretched victim of this practical joke was in the greatest danger, and his voice could be heard amidst the smoke crying out for mercy. Water was dashed on to the trunk, but only increased the danger by augmenting the smoke; and the resinous properties of the pine rendered all efforts to subdue the flames unavailing. Most providentially another tree grew close at hand, into which, at the imminent risk of being dashed to pieces, the victim leaped, and succeeded in grasping a bough, where he hung until another man climbed up and rescued him. On the 1st of June the *Tonquin* sailed for the north, having Mr. McKay on board as supercargo, and Mr. Lewis as ship's clerk, but as Captain Thorn had sent Mr. Mumford, the second mate, on shore, the ship was very short of officers.

"At the time of the vessel's sailing the settlement was almost defenceless, no palisade had been erected, and not a single gun was mounted, whilst the Indians swarmed round in such numbers that the people had to relinquish all labour and think only of their own safety. The good offices of the crafty Comecomly were sought in this emergency, and on the promise of a reward he established friendly communications between the traders and the Indians, who at length went away, apparently satisfied with the reception they had experienced. An accident, however, nearly marred the existing harmony. Mr. McDougall had invited a Chinook chief to his tent, and was explaining to him the nature and properties of a blunderbuss, when by some accident the hammer fell and the weapon exploded, blowing off the corner of the chief's robe, and only missing his body by a miracle. Out darted the affrighted potentate, yelling to his followers, who replied by the dreaded war whoop. During this time the sentinel seeing smoke issue from the tent, and the chief bolting at full speed, thought the latter had murdered Mr. McDougall, and fired at him, calling out to the other white men, who seizing their arms hastened to the spot with their fingers on the trigger, and a very pretty fight seemed imminent. McDougall, however, and Mr. Ross, who luckily was in the tent at the time, both rushed between the hostile ranks, and peace was at length restored, though the chief was a long time before he got rid of the idea that a plot had been formed against his life.

" Two strange Indians, a man and woman, now made their appearance at the fort—for the building was progressing—who described themselves as coming from the Rocky Mountains, and spoke the Algonquin language; but in the middle of July the Astorians were astonished at seeing a light bark canoe sweeping down the Columbia, which was found to contain Mr. Thompson, of the North-West Company, with a crew of eight Iroquois Indians and an interpreter. Of course the new comers had no very friendly feelings towards the American Company, and Thompson tried to discourage the Astorians in every way, by painting the difficulties and dangers they would encounter if they persevered in their attempts to establish a trade. According to Thompson's account, he had left Canada in the preceding year, with a considerable party and plenty of goods, intending to cross the Rocky Mountains. The majority of his men had deserted him when real hardships had to be faced, but he had persisted in pushing on with the few who had remained faithful to him, and had reached the source of the Columbia, where his Indians had built the bark canoe. The real truth was, that immediately on hearing of Mr. Astor's scheme, the North-West Company took the alarm, and resolved to anticipate him by establishing a post on the Columbia river themselves. Mr. Thompson was therefore despatched overland with a large party, and all the necessary appliances, but his men deserting him, the project had failed. He was, however, a man of wonderful energy, and visited many Indian villages, presenting their inhabitants with English flags, some of which he even planted in the forks of the rivers, claiming the country in the name of the king for the great association to which he belonged. The misconduct of his men having frustrated his hopes of anticipating the Astorians, he had come down the river to reconnoitre the enemy's camp.

" Mr. McDougall received Mr. Thompson very

kindly, and listened with much attention to the account of all the misfortunes so confidently predicted by the latter, though there is little reason to suppose these took deep root, for most of the Astorians were old North-Westers themselves, and knew exactly how much to believe and how much to discredit. Mr. Thompson announced his intention of returning in a few days to Canada by the same route that he had come, and this was thought by McDougall a fitting opportunity for sending out a small expedition to establish a trading post in the interior; and the two parties agreed to proceed in company for the sake of mutual protection. The Astorians told off for this undertaking were Messrs. David Stuart, Ross, Pillelte, McLennan, my father, two other *voyageurs*, and two Sandwich Islanders, and on the 22nd July, 1811, they left the factory, accompanied by Mr. Thompson's party and the two strange Indians I mentioned before. Unlike the light bark canoes to which he had been accustomed, the craft in which my father now found himself was a clumsy Chinook dug-out, deeply laden with goods for the Indian trade. For nearly a hundred miles the course of the river was about south-east, and the canoes made the best of their way against a strong current. On one occasion they passed a small rocky height called Mount Coffin, which was completely covered with canoes of all sizes and descriptions, used by the fishing Indians as receptacles for their dead. As far as Point Vancouver, which is about one hundred and ten miles from the bar, the Columbia is navigable for vessels of four hundred tons, and here the tidal influence ceases to be perceptible. At last the foot of the Cascades was reached, and it became necessary to make a portage. They had no sooner landed than a great number of Indians presented themselves, and became troublesome from their continual demands for presents. The distribution of a few trinkets amongst the chiefs brought them to order, and then the transport of the goods commenced by a most abominable path fifteen hundred yards in length, and mounting up and down steep banks throughout its whole distance. Had all the men been like my father and the other two *voyageurs*, they would have made short work of such a trumpery affair, but they were wholly unaccustomed to such a thing, and it was sunset by the time everything was safely crossed.

"A ludicrous incident happened to one of the party, Mr. Ross, which always amused my father. Being unused to carry, he was deputed to stand as sentinel at the lower end of the portage below the Cascades, where the canoes were secured; but seeing his companions quite exhausted with the hard work, Ross seized a roll of tobacco, and started off to carry it himself. By the time the top of the first steep bank was reached, the severe nature of his self-imposed task became apparent, and he stood recovering his breath, when an Indian passed, to whom he offered all the buttons on his coat if he would convey the parcel across in safety. After some demur the fellow acceded, and catching up the roll, started off at speed, Mr. Ross following him as best he could ; but when they had arrived nearly at the other end, the Indian pitched the parcel down a precipice two hundred feet in height, and left the white man to recover it as best he could. Mr. Ross had nothing left for it but to scramble down first, and then scramble up with the tobacco on his shoulders, during which performance he was greeted with roars of laughter by the Indian and by some fifty of his tribe, whom he had summoned to witness the success of his little joke ; but what added insult to injury was that the rascal insisted on being paid, and claimed the buttons, which, rather than embroil the party with the natives, Mr. Ross gave up.

"You admire beautiful scenery, I know, Monsieur Paul, therefore I shall tell you about the falls of the Columbia River. I was there myself for many weeks only a few years ago, so what I tell you now is from my own observation. The rapids commence by a perpendicular pitch of at least twenty feet over which the water falls in a green wall, only the lip of which is visible from the cloud of ascending spray. The troubled waters now dash down an inclined plane of a mile in length amidst islands of black rock, and then arrive at another cascade of less than ten feet in height which is divided by two rocks. About two miles below this second fall the river widens out into a huge basin surrounded by a perpendicular wall of black rock, from which its waters seem to have no escape, for the outlet is invisible. To the left of this rocky barrier, however, a chasm forty five yards in width gives a passage to the river, which tears down the confined space in a seething mass of foam, through which, however, canoes skilfully handled can pass, for I have taken one down myself frequently. A mile and a half from the end of this channel is a rapid, formed by two rocky islands ; and two miles beyond a ledge of rocks extends from shore to shore forming another cascade twenty feet in height, after which the river is hurried through another long but confined channel for the distance of three miles ; this last race is called the 'Long Narrows,' and is the great salmon ground of the

M

Columbia. After the winter, when the river is well flushed with water, the fish ascend from the sea in countless thousands, and as they worm their way upward through the 'Narrows' the natives, standing on stages projecting over the torrent, catch them in hoop nets, and fling them in hundreds on to the shore. Here the squaws are in readiness to clean them, after which they are placed in the sun on scaffolds planted along the river banks. When sufficiently dry, they are cured in a peculiar manner, being pounded fine between two stones, pressed, and finally packed in grass matting.

" My father and his companions found the Cascade Indians thievish and troublesome, and it was only by the exercise of great forbearance that a rupture was avoided. They stole an axe, notwithstanding the sharp look-out that was kept, and a whole suit of clothes belonging to Mr. McLennan, who, standing up in the canoe, threw the hat amongst them, that the whole suit might be complete. Above the Cascades the river resumes its usual breadth and appearance, and for several hundred miles the two parties kept together; but at last the time arrived for Mr. Thompson to push on by himself, and one of his men wishing to join the Astorians, who could speak Indian, and would be of great use to them, an exchange was effected, and with a light heart, my father, after shaking hands with his companions, took his seat in the beautiful birch-bark canoe and once more turned his face towards Canada, too glad to wash his hands of Astoria, and to be again in the service of the North-West Company. After a pleasant journey, for it was in the autumn, my father found himself once more at Montreal, after such an experience of the blue ocean that he never could be induced to go eastward of Quebec until the day of his death."

" But, Pierre, your father's return cuts the story rather short. What became of the factory and the *Tonquin*, and was Captain Thorn ever brought to justice for his brutality ?"

" I hardly know the whole circumstances of the case, Monsieur Paul, but I believe the *Tonquin* was burned, and I know that Astoria was made over to the North-West Company. Nothing pleased my father better than to tell so much of the settlement as he saw, and it is owing to hearing it many times that I remember it so well. But in what took place afterwards he was not much interested."

As, however, my readers may differ from Baptiste Lefranc, I shall give them a brief outline of the remaining history of Astoria and of the fate of Captain Thorn and his vessel.

M 2

CHAPTER IX.

R. STUART established a station at Oakanagan, and in due time the overland party, after encountering the most fearful hardships, chiefly on the west side of the Rocky Mountains, arrived at Astoria, where rumours were already rife of the loss of the *Tonquin*. The account of that terrible catastrophe to the infant settlement is thus reported by an Indian named Kasiascall, or Lamazu, who had witnessed the whole affair.

Pierre Lefranc said that the *Tonquin* left Astoria on the 1st of June, which was the case, but owing to contrary winds she was prevented from crossing the bar at the mouth of the river until the 5th. The number of persons then on board was twenty-three, inclusive of Messrs. McKay and Lewis. Shortly after leaving the Columbia, the *Tonquin* anchored for the night in a small bay, and was there boarded by a canoe containing several Indians, one of whom was Lamazu, and as this man had been engaged in former voyages along the coast, and was acquainted with the languages of the various tribes, the supercargo, Mr. McKay, asked him to accompany the vessel, to which he agreed, and his scanty effects having been transferred from the canoe to the *Tonquin*, Captain Thorn weighed anchor and stood to the northward. In a few days the harbour of Neweetu, in Vancouver's Island, was reached, and, contrary to the advice of Lamazu, who knew the treacherous character of the natives, the captain brought to for the purpose of trading. Numbers of canoes soon surrounded the ship; but as the day was too far advanced to commence business, Mr. McKay and the interpreter (Lamazu) went ashore to the village of the chief, Wicananish, where the former was received with great hospitality, and passed the night on a bed of sea-otter skins especially prepared for his accommodation in the lodge of the chief. Lamazu returned to the vessel.

So far the Indian was unwavering in his story; but at this point he gave two different accounts of the insult offered to the natives by which their vengeance was drawn down upon the fated *Tonquin*. Which of the man's statements is correct there is no means of knowing, either or both might be partly true, and by recording each the reader can judge for himself.

One account is, that on the following morning, while the supercargo was still ashore, the natives came off in great numbers, headed by the two sons of Wicananish. They had with them many valuable sea-otter skins, and, eager to secure these, Captain Thorn did not wait for McKay's return, but commenced the trade himself, having first spread out on the deck knives, blankets, fish-hooks, and such other articles as he thought likely to tempt his customers. The Indians, however, had been accustomed to dealing with Europeans, and were far from being the simple and credulous people Captain Thorn supposed; there was also amongst their number an old chief named Nookmis, who knew the value of each article as well as the skipper himself, and from this veteran the other Indians seemed to take their cue, rejecting Thorn's offers with scorn, and demanding at least double for their furs. This conduct was highly displeasing to the captain, whose temper was, as we know, none of the best; so, ceasing to bargain with the natives, he thrust his hands deep into his pockets, and walked the deck in sullen silence. Whilst thus engaged, he was followed step by step by Nookmis, who held a sea-otter skin in his hand, and pestered the angry man to trade. As importunty elicited no reply, the old Indian tried other means, and commenced bantering Thorn on the low prices he offered. This caused the volcano slumbering in the captain's breast to break forth with a vengeance, and snatching the skin from the hands of his tormentor, he first rubbed it in his face, and then kicked him over the ship's side, returning to do the same with the other bundles of peltry, which were soon flying in all directions urged by the foot of the exasperated skipper. The old chief hurried ashore speechless with rage at the insult, and soon every Indian had left the ship, some of them vowing vengeance for so gross an indignity.

Such is one version of the story given by Lamazu, We now pass on to the second.

Here he states that McKay did not sleep at the chief's house, but returned on board that evening, having seen many sea-otter skins. On the following day the Indians came off in great numbers to trade, and on seeing them Captain Thorn ordered the boarding nettings to be triced up round the ship, and gave directions that only ten natives should be allowed on board at once. These precautions carried out, trade commenced ; but in a few minutes the captain observed an Indian making an opening in the boarding netting with his knife, to enable him to slip on board. Directly this man saw that he was detected, he jumped into a canoe and escaped, upon which the captain told the chiefs to call him back, but they smiled and said nothing, which so exasperated the headstrong man that he collared two of the chiefs and threatened to hang them unless the offender was delivered up for punishment. The moment this seizure was made the Indians fled, and the two chiefs remained on board as prisoners, having a guard placed over them. Though food and drink were offered to them, they refused to taste either, and showed unmistakably the resentment they felt at such harsh treatment. On the following day the delinquent was brought off in a canoe, and delivered up to the captain, who had him stripped and seized up to the gratings, but stopped short of flogging him. Both the chiefs and the prisoner were now released, and all left the ship, the former disdainfully refusing a present that was offered them, and vowing vengeance for the insults to which they had been subjected.

The above is the second account of the manner in which Captain Thorn turned friends into deadly enemies, and whichever may be the correct one, it remains undoubted that the harshness and cruelty of the commander contributed greatly to the disastrous end which befell the ship and her crew,

whilst his stubborn disregard of all advice enabled
the natives to execute their scheme of vengeance
unchecked. I now proceed with the thread of the
story.

The interpreter spoke to Mr. McKay, and begged
him to use his influence with the captain for the
removal of the ship from such dangerous quarters,
adding that he was well acquainted with the
temper of the natives, and felt confident that they
would show their resentment in some signal manner.
In the justice of this the supercargo, who had
himself gained a great insight into Indian character,
perfectly coincided, and joining the captain, he
urged him to get up the anchor and leave Newcetu;
but his advice was made light of, and the skipper
pointed to the guns and fire-arms which he held
sufficient to beat off the whole tribe, and wound up
by many taunting remarks to the remonstrances of
the supercargo. No Indians showed themselves
during that day, but at daybreak on the following
morning, before the captain and Mr. McKay had
risen, a canoe manned with twenty Indians under
the command of Shewish, a son of the chief
Wicananish, came alongside, and holding up sea-
otter skins they intimated their wish to trade. The
officer in charge of the deck, seeing that their
demeanour was friendly, and that they were

unarmed, permitted them to come on board; and
shortly afterwards several other canoes followed,
and the ship was thronged with natives. The
officer in charge now felt some alarm, and running
down below, called the captain and Mr. McKay,
who speedily appeared upon deck; when the former,
perhaps anxious to atone for his previous insults,
received the chiefs with protestations of friendship,
and neglected to observe the precautions usual in
the Indian traffic, though their observance had
been repeatedly impressed upon him by Mr. Astor
both by word of mouth and by letter. In his
instructions Captain Thorn was enjoined "to be
courteous and kind in his dealings with the savages,
but by no means to confide in their apparent
friendship, *nor to admit more than a few on board
of his ship at a time."* How he obeyed the first
part of these orders has been already related; we
now come to the consequences of his total disregard
of the second.

Notwithstanding that the natives were apparently
unarmed, the interpreter noticed that they all wore
short fur mantles, under which it was quite possible
that weapons might be concealed; and mentioning
his suspicion to Mr. McKay, that gentleman urged
the captain to clear the ship and get under weigh;
but he took no notice of the warning until the

increasing number of canoes that surrounded the vessel, whose dusky occupants were now roving at will about every part of the deck, seemed to awaken his distrust, and he sent some men aloft to loose the sails ; whilst the remainder manned the windlass and commenced heaving in the cable.

Seeing that the departure of the ship was resolved upon, the Indians pretended to yield to the captain's prices, and a brisk trade ensued without any haggling or demur on the part of the natives, who parted freely with their skins for knives, and thus they became possessed of for- midable weapons in addition to those concealed beneath their robes

Whilst this hurried barter was proceeding, the anchor had been hove nearly to the bows and the sails loosed, therefore the captain gave orders to clear the ship, shouting his command in a loud peremptory voice which was heard the length and breadth of the vessel, and was instantly answered by the war-whoop of the savages, whose newly- purchased knives and concealed war-clubs were brandished aloft as they rushed upon the doomed Europeans. Mr. Lewis, the ship's clerk, who was leaning with folded arms over a bale of blankets, fell first, receiving, whilst bargaining with a native, a treacherous stab in the back from another, which precipitated him headlong down the hatchway. The supercargo, whose life it is believed the Indians wished to spare, for he was a great favourite, fell next, knocked over the taffrail by a club, and despatched while in the water by the squaws who were left in the canoes.

On all sides the captain found himself assailed, and great as were his faults, his lion-like courage was even greater. He was a man of a powerful muscular frame, and from always having despised the Indians was never in the habit of carrying arms, so on this occasion he was without any weapon, except a clasp knife which he snatched from the merchandise exposed for barter. But even with this miserable instrument he proved a formidable antagonist. At the first outbreak, Shewish, old Wicananish's son, had marked the captain for his prey, and rushed furiously upon him, only to reel back lifeless, stabbed to the heart. The followers of the young chief now assailed him, but the number of dead and wounded bodies with which the deck was strewn, testified to the vigour of his resistance. Though bleeding from many wounds the gallant man—one feels inclined to forgive him all on reading of his heroism—strove to reach his cabin, in which stood the loaded fire-arms, and he had nearly succeeded in fighting his way through the circle of his enemies. Another step, and the hatchway would be reached; but faint from loss of blood, he leant for one brief moment against the tiller. A savage standing behind brought his war-club down with the full swing of his brawny arm upon the sailor's unguarded head, and even before he reached the deck a dozen thirsty knives were sheathed in his body, which was hurried to the side and flung over board.

Whilst these bloody deeds were being perpetrated on the quarter-deck, a desperate struggle was taking place throughout the ship wherever a white man could be found. The sailors resisted manfully with whatever weapons they could seize, and many a savage fell lifeless to the deck before the sweep of the handspikes with which the windlass had just been worked; but the struggle was of short duration, for the poor fellows were outnumbered, and one by one they yielded up their lives before the blows and stabs of their enemies.

During the brief space that the above transactions really occupied, the seven men who had been sent aloft to loose the sails, witnessing the carnage below, attempted to get between decks by sliding down the running rigging. Three fell in the attempt — one of them, Stephen Weekes, the armourer, whose narrow escape from drowning on the bar was told by Pierre Lefranc—but the remaining four managed to reach the cabin, in which they found Mr. Lewis, still alive, and endeavouring to stanch the blood flowing from the mortal wound between his shoulders. Dragging all the cabin furniture to the door, the four men soon made a rough barricade, and having possessed themselves of the muskets and ammunition, they broke open the companion hatch, and through the holes, opened a fire on the exulting savages, now engaged in the congenial occupation of plundering the stores, that soon cleared the deck and forced the miscreants to take shelter in their canoes. The interpreter leaped overboard whilst the carnage was at its height, and was picked up by the women in the canoes, into which the survivors, the moment the savages shoved off, discharged the cannon with which the *Tonquin* was armed, and committed great destruction. No Indians ventured off to the ship that day nor during the succeeding night. Lamazu's narrative as an eye-witness ends here, and I therefore quote the remainder of this tragical history from Mr. Washington Irving, who had access to all Mr. Astor's papers.

"When the day dawned the *Tonquin* still lay at anchor in the bay, her sails all loose and flapping in the wind, and no one apparently on board of her. After a time, some of the canoes ventured forth to reconnoitre, taking with them the interpreter. They paddled about her, keeping cautiously at a distance, but growing more and more imboldened at seeing her quiet and lifeless. One man at length made his appearance on the deck, and was recognised by the interpreter as Mr. Lewis. He made friendly signs, and invited them on board. It was long before they ventured to comply. Those who mounted the deck met with no opposition ; no one was to be seen on board, for Mr. Lewis, after inviting them, had disappeared. Other canoes now pressed forward to board the prize ; the decks were soon crowded, and the sides covered with clambering savages, all intent on plunder. In the midst of their eagerness and exultation the ship blew up with a tremendous explosion. Arms, legs, and mutilated bodies were blown into the air, and dreadful havoc was made in the surrounding canoes. The interpreter was in the main chains at the time of the explosion, and was thrown unhurt into the water, where he succeeded in getting into one of the canoes. According to his statement, the bay presented an awful spectacle after the catastrophe. The ship had disappeared, but the bay was covered with fragments of the wreck, with shattered canoes, and Indians swimming for their lives, or struggling in the agonies of death ; while those who had escaped the danger remained aghast and stupefied, or made with frantic panic for the shore.   Upwards of a hundred savages were destroyed by the explosion, many more were shockingly mutilated, and for days afterwards the limbs and bodies of the slain were thrown upon the beach.

"The inhabitants of Newestee (Newcetu) were overwhelmed with consternation at this astounding calamity, which had burst upon them in the very moment of triumph.   The warriors sat mute and mournful, while the women filled the air with loud lamentations.   Their weeping and wailing, however, was suddenly changed into yells of fury at the sight of four unfortunate white men, brought captive into the village.   They had been driven on shore in one of the ship's boats, and taken at some distance along the coast.

"The interpreter was permitted to converse with them.   They proved to be the four brave fellows who had made such desperate defence from the cabin.   The interpreter gathered from them some of the particulars already related.   They told him further, that, after they had beaten off the enemy, and cleared the ship, Lewis advised that they should slip the cable and endeavour to get to sea. They declined to take his advice, alleging that the wind set too strongly into the bay, and would drive them on shore. They resolved, as soon as it was dark, to put off quietly in the ship's boat, which they would be able to do unperceived, and to coast along back to Astoria. They put their resolution into effect; but Lewis refused to accompany them, being disabled by his wound, hopeless of escape, and determined on a terrible revenge. On the voyage out he had repeatedly expressed a presentiment that he should die by his own hands; thinking it highly probable that he should be engaged in some contest with the natives, and being resolved, in case of extremity, to commit suicide rather than be made a prisoner. He now declared his intention to remain on board the ship until daylight, to decoy as many of the savages on board as possible, then to set fire to the powder magazine, and terminate his life by a signal act of vengeance. How well he succeeded has been shown. His companions bade him a melancholy adieu, and set off on their precarious expedition. They strove with might and main to get out of the bay, but found it impossible to weather a point of land, and were at length compelled to take shelter in a small cove, where they hoped to remain concealed until

N

the wind became more favourable.   Exhausted by fatigue and watching, they fell into a sound sleep, and in that state were surprised by the savages.   Better had it been for those unfortunate men had they remained with Lewis, and shared his heroic death ; as it was, they perished in a more lingering and protracted manner, being sacrificed by the natives to the manes of their friends with all the lingering tortures of savage cruelty.   Some time after their death, the interpreter, who had remained a kind of prisoner at large, effected his escape, and brought the tragical tidings to Astoria."

So says Washington Irving, but Mr. Alexander Ross, who was an Astorian, and one of the passengers in the *Tonquin*, writes: " Thus ended the sad story of Kasiascall (Lamazu), a story which we at the time believed to be perfectly true ; but not many days after, some Indians belonging to the same quarter reached Astoria also, and gave a somewhat different version of the affair, particularly as regarded Kasiascall himself ; and what convinced us that he had acted a treacherous part, was the fact, that on hearing that the other Indians were coming, he immediately absconded, and we saw him no more.   These Indians confirmed Kasiascall's story in every respect as regarded the destruction of the ill fated *Tonquin ;* but persisted in assuring

us that he was not on board at the time, and that
he was privy to the whole plot. They said, that
before that affair he had caused the death of four
white men, and that early in the morning of the
Tonquin's fatal day, he had induced the captain,
through some plausible artifice, to send a boat with
six men to shore, and that neither he nor the six
men were on board at the time of the destruction.
That in the evening of the same day, Kasiascall
himself headed the party who went and brought
the **six** unfortunate men, after the ship was
blown up, to the Indian camp, where they were
first tortured with savage cruelty, and then all
massacred in the most inhuman manner."

Such was the fate of the *Tonquin*, as accurately
as it can be ascertained, and there is no doubt that
the story is substantially true. I now pass on to
the settlement at Astoria.

CHAPTER X.

AFTER the sailing of the *Tonquin* and before the arrival of the overland party under Mr. Hunt, the settlers at the mouth of the Columbia River had much cause for anxiety. The departure of Mr. David Stuart and his party for the establishment of a trading station on the Oakanagan had weakened their numbers, and the Indians seemed well aware of this, for they ceased to visit Astoria, and rumours of a coalition of the various tribes in the vicinity for its destruction became rife. But the resolute little band were equal to the emergency, and by hard work had in a few days thrown up temporary defences, surrounding the warehouses and habitations with a strong palisade, flanked by two bastions, on which a couple of small cannon were mounted. All the men were also drilled daily, exercised in the use of arms, and familiarised with the part they would have to play in case of an attack, to guard against which sentinels kept a vigilant watch night and day. When the news of the *Tonquin's* loss reached them, their hearts fell, for many valuable stores belonging to the settlement were destroyed in the vessel, Captain Thorn having proposed to land them on his return from the North, by which time suitable buildings would have been prepared for their reception ; now they saw themselves, a mere handful of men, bereft of the supplies on which they had relied, and encompassed on every side by daring and treacherous foes.

At this juncture Mr. McDougall had resource to a device that reflects credit on his powers of invention. Some years previously the small-pox— that fatal gift of the white man, by which whole tribes of their red brethren have been exterminated —had broken out, and ravaged the wild regions west of the Rocky Mountains. Though it had now fulfilled its destructive mission and had died out, the Indians were in daily dread of its re-appearance, the knowledge of which prompted the governor of Astoria to practice on their credulity in the following manner. He summoned the chiefs whom he believed most deeply implicated in the conspiracy against the white men, entertained them hospitably and then made them a speech. He said that he was fully aware of the loss of the *Tonquin*, and of the treachery of the Vancouver Island tribes, for the punishment of which he had determined on a terrible revenge. "The white men among you," he added with solemnity, "are but as the mountains, while you are like the sands of the sea in number; nevertheless the white men are strong to punish, for they possess a mighty medicine. Look at this bottle," and he produced a small phial tightly stoppered; "it is small and insignificant to the eye, but you would hardly sit so quietly, perhaps meditating treason in your hearts, were you aware of its contents. In this little vessel," raising both his voice and the bottle, "I hold safely corked up the scourge of your nation—the dreaded small-pox; if I dash it to the ground, the pestilence will fly forth north, south, east and west, and the red man, his squaws, his children, and his kindred will perish miserably from off the face of the earth!"

The awe-stricken listeners sat mute with terror and dismay, and when they found their voices, it was to implore the mercy and forbearance of the great medicine-man, urging that the disease, if once let out, would punish both the guilty and the guiltless alike, and appealing to his justice not to submit both to so terrible a doom. Of course, after much persuasion, Mr. McDougall was induced to put the fatal bottle safely away, but he gave them plainly to understand that at the first act of hostility it should be uncorked, and the affrighted natives departed, having bestowed upon the wily Scotchman the title of "the great small-pox chief."

Danger being removed by this artifice, the settlers continued building and strengthening their factory, and also put together the little schooner, whose frame had been landed from the *Tonquin*. She was christened the *Dolly*, and launched with much ceremony on the 2nd of October, 1811. The year gradually wore away, the winter rains beat down pitilessly and furiously on Astoria, swelling brooks into rivers, and the river into a mighty surging sea. The last day of December came, and still no relief had reached them, save only four men whom gallant David Stuart had sent down from the Oakanagan, remaining in that lonely wilderness with only Mr. Ross and two other subordinates. On that closing day of the year the rain, as out of pity, ceased, and the new year was heralded by a glorious sunshine, at sight of which the hearts of the lonely men were warmed, and with the aid of a little extra rum and flour a feast and dance were got up, and amidst the firing of cannon and other harmless festivities the infant 1812 was ushered in.

Into all the particulars of the overland expedition under Mr. Hunt I am unable to enter here, but can only say that history presents few records of danger and privation more cheerfully endured. The whole account reads more like a thrilling romance than the stern reality it actually was. During their eventful journey they suffered from almost every hardship that humanity can endure and still survive—from pirates, from hostile Indians, some of whom had the painted semblance of a red hand across their mouths, a sign that they had drunk the life blood of a foe! from weakness and disease, from the heavy hand of gaunt starvation. A touching story indeed! Perishing from hunger, the party had broken up into several sections on the western slope of the Rocky Mountains, and each had striven to reach Astoria as best it could. No want of unanimity or lack of confidence in their gallant leader caused this division; it was enforced by the poverty of the country, which did not carry sufficient game or roots for the whole band. On the 15th of February the main body, under Mr. Hunt, swept round an intervening cape in their canoes, and came in sight of the settlement. Their historian thus describes it: "After eleven months' wandering in the wilderness, a great part of the time over trackless wastes, where the sight of a savage wigwam was a rarity, we may imagine the delight of the poor weather-beaten travellers at

MACLELLAN STALKS THE BIG-HORN.

Page 207.

beholding the embryo establishment, with its mag-
azines, habitations, and picketed bulwarks, seated
on a high point of land, dominating a beautiful
little bay, in which was a trim-built shallop lying
quietly at anchor. A shout of joy burst from each
canoe at the long-wished-for sight. They urged
their canoes across the bay, and pulled with eagerness for shore, where all hands poured down from
the settlements to receive and welcome them.
Among the first to greet them on their landing
were some of their old comrades and fellow-sufferers, who, under the conduct of Reed, McLellan,
and McKenzie, had parted with them at the
Caldron Linn. These had reached Astoria nearly
a month previously, and, judging from their own
narrow escape from starvation, had given up Mr.
Hunt and his followers as lost. Their greeting was
the more warm and cordial. As to the Canadian
voyageurs, their mutual felicitations, as usual, were
loud and vociferous, and it was almost ludicrous to
behold these ancient 'comrades' and 'confreres'
hugging and kissing each other on the river bank."

The different parties now exchanged an account
of their adventures, all of which were eventful
enough, but I must content myself by describing
the proceedings of one, which will give the reader
some idea of the rest.

Three exploring parties had set off in different directions, and after wandering for several days in search of game or Indians, neither of which they found, had all accidentally met among the Snake River mountains. They now numbered eleven, namely, Messrs. McLellan, McKenzie, Reed, and eight men, chiefly Canadians. Being all equally destitute, and without horses, provisions, or information, the little band resolved to push their own way to the Columbia River in place of returning to Mr. Hunt and becoming a further drag on his already painfully scanty resources. In accordance with this self-devoted project they made their way down the course of the Snake River, scaling precipices and traversing a frightfully rugged country, in whose every feature was legibly written famine and misery.

Though close to the river, and often within sight of its sparkling flood, their greatest enemy was thirst, for the precipitous banks prevented them reaching the waters beneath, whose babbling murmur added tenfold to their agony. Nor was hunger absent to alleviate in some measure their misery. Not a head of game could be met with, and for some days their only subsistence was strips of beaver-skin, warmed through on the ashes. Weary, fainting, and dejected, they crept slowly onward, meeting at rare intervals a little rain-water which had lodged in the crevice of a rock, and which just sufficed to keep body and soul together. At length a severe snow storm came on, and brought them to a standstill, for in their enfeebled condition any attempt to struggle through it was useless, and convinced of this the wanderers gathered under the shelter of a rock, and there seated themselves in readiness for the death that they deemed inevitable.

Resignedly at the base of that rock, beneath the shadow of a gloomy mountain, those eleven men prepared to die—to leave their bones bleaching in the rugged wilderness after their flesh had gone to feed the wolf and the raven. Even the light-hearted Canadians felt the influence of the impending doom, and the ready jest and smile with which they had lightened many a weary hour were absent, and replaced by a muttered prayer to the Throne on high or the meaningless glance of blank despair. But suddenly McLellan, who from the position he had taken up could command a greater extent of the surrounding landscape than his companions, motioned them to silence, and with outstretched arm pointed to a big-horn or Rocky Mountain sheep, that had taken shelter under a shelving rock on the side of the hill above them.

Hope was now visible in each haggard face, and

with the utmost caution McLellan, who was an excellent shot, and a man of iron nerve, seized his rifle, and crawled away to try and stalk the wary animal. His splendid frame had withstood the privations to which they had been subjected better than those of the other men, thus he was best fitted for the toilsome task, and like a snake he crept away amidst the snow, and was soon lost to sight. By an effort of imagination we can perhaps conjure up the sight of those twenty eyes eagerly fixed upon the big-horn, and viewing with despair its slightest change of position. If the sheep raised its fore foot or shook its armed head a tremor ran through the ranks, for might not the movement precede departure?

" Surely he has had time to make a safe circuit and ascend the hill?" whispered one of the most impatient, and as though in answer to his almost inaudible question, the sharp crack of a rifle rang through the silent valley, and with one convulsive bound into the air the big-horn fell dead, shot straight through the heart.

And now the pent-up feelings of each man found vent, and cheers, feeble but heartfelt, greeted the resolute hunter as he emerged from his hiding-place, and creeping to the ledge on which the slain animal lay, rolled its body down the hill to his companions beneath. Owing to McLellan's nerve their lives were saved. Had he only wounded the big-horn it must have escaped, for not one of the party was capable of pursuing it.

The animal was soon cut up, but with wonderful self-denial the starving men reserved all the meat for future occasions, and contented themselves with soup made out of the bones. Strengthened in body and elated in spirit by this manifestation of Providence on their behalf, the wanderers pursued their weary way, and ultimately, after three weeks of suffering and unremitting toil, during the course of which they were several times reduced to almost the same straits, they escaped from the mountains and arrived at Lewis River, a tributary of the Columbia. Here they met with wild horses, and encountered a tribe of friendly Indians, who received them with much kindness, and supplied every want that lay within their power, giving them, amongst other things, two canoes, in which they made their way to Astoria, arriving at the settlement, haggard, enfeebled, emaciated, and with only a few miserable rags in the shape of clothing.

This was the account given by one party, and from it the reader may form some idea of the others. All the overlanders had now reached Astoria, with the exception of six, Mr. Crooks,

John Day, a Kentucky hunter, and four Canadians, and the Astorians held high jubilee in honour of the occasion ; the American colours were run up to the flag-staff, the cannon fired ; fish and venison smoked upon the board ; a plentiful allowance of rum was distributed ; and a ball, given by the Canadian *voyageurs* lasted far into the small hours of the following morning.

Spring once more reigned over the country on the Columbia, and now the Astorians bestirred themselves, for there were many things to be done, and several expeditions to send forth. In the first place, Mr. David Stuart must be visited at the lonely little station on the Oakanagan, where he and Mr. Ross had passed the winter ; secondly, many articles of value cached, or secretly hidden, by Mr. Hunt's party, had to be recovered ; and lastly, despatches to Mr. Astor, informing him of the condition of the settlement, had to be sent overland to New York.

The first of these enterprises was confided to Mr. Robert Stuart, a nephew of the gentleman at Oakanagan ; two clerks were entrusted with the second ; whilst the third and most dangerous was willingly accepted by Mr. Reed, who, the reader may remember, was one of the party on the Snake River. With only three men, Reed was to make

the long and toilsome journey over the entire continent, and the first step he took—he was an Irish-
man—was to have a tin box constructed for his
despatches, and this he slung over his shoulder,
vowing only to surrender it with his life.

As these different parties would all pursue the
same route for several hundred miles, it was resolved
that they should start together, for mutual protection at the Cascades, where the Indians were of a
piratical disposition, and always gave much trouble;
and I should here mention that when Mr. McLellan
heard that Reed was returning to the States, he
. resolved on accompanying him, to which no oppo-·
sition was offered by the other partners, for this
gentleman was of a most decided character, and was
dissatisfied with the share he held in the Company.

Accordingly, the brigade of canoes started under
the command of Mr. Robert Stuart, and early in
the month of April arrived at the Long Narrows,
where both canoes and goods had to be transported
by land, and the assistance of some Indians were
called in to effect this. These vagabonds made off
with some of the property, and pilfered at every
opportunity, resolving above all things to captuie
Reed's tin box, which shone brilliantly in the sun,
and which they supposed, from the solicitude with
which its owner guarded it, contained "a great

medicine." Determined to circumvent these pirates,
Mr. Stuart proposed that they should all make an
effort to convey the goods across during the night,
when the suspicious robbers would be sleeping, and
so well was this manœuvre executed that when day
dawned only two boat-loads remained to be carried
over. The men were despatched with one of these,
and Messrs. Reed and McLellan remained to guard
the other until their return. But alas! the glitter of
the "great medicine" suspended from the Irish-
man's back caught the eyes of the Indians, who,
yelling out the war-whoop, sprang upon their prey.
After the fash:on of his countrymen this gentleman .
had carefully covered the lock of his rifle when he
was most likely to want it, and whilst endeavouring
to remove the obstacle, a blow on the head from a
war-club stretched him senseless, and in the
twinkling of an eye his active assailants had gained
possession of his rifle, pistol, and tin box, with
which they made off as fast as their legs would
carry them. In the mean time some of the other
savages made an attempt on the goods guarded by
McLellan, and one of their number advancing
towards that gentleman, endeavoured to fling his
buffalo robe in his eyes with one hand, and to stab
him with the other; but McLellan was too quick
for him, he saw the meditated treachery, and

springing backwards clear of the blow, shot his assailant dead on the spot.

Affairs would have gone badly with the two whites had the Indians not raised the war-whoop; but luckily Mr. Stuart was at no great distance, and, hearing the yell, hurried back with half a dozen men, to find Reed lying in a pool of his own blood, while an Indian was bending over in the act of despatching him with a tomahawk. A rifle ball from a Kentucky trapper laid the savage low, and the men then charged the Indians, who fled in all directions. Carrying Reed with them, the party then hurried to the upper end of the portage, and embarked in their canoes amidst the yells and war-whoops of the exasperated natives.

Paddling with all their strength, the white men continued their journey along the southern bank of the river, whilst the Indians returned to the scene of action, and removed their two friends, one of whom was still living, to the village. Here they roused themselves to a proper pitch of frenzy by killing two horses, whose blood they drank, and by dancing around the corpse of the slain man, and then, having painted themselves for battle, mounted their horses, and started off with the intention of getting ahead of the canoes, which they hoped to surprise, and then to take a terrible reverge on the

O

whites. This they partially succeeded in doing, but were discovered whilst crossing the river, and the Astorians, lashing their canoes together, waited the impending attack.

Presently they perceived a canoe approaching, in which were seated the chief and three of his bravest warriors, who came to hold a parley. They said that one of their number had been killed and another wounded, and that the relatives of both these men cried out for vengeance. They themselves were anxious to avoid all bloodshed, so if the whites would just hand over Mr. Reed—who was only a shade better than a dead man now—to be tortured and put to death, they would settle matters so that the relatives should be satisfied, and the war-hatchet could be buried without any further trouble.

To this modest demand, so gratifying in its very nature to poor Reed, an indignant refusal was of course returned, and the chief withdrew with his warriors to hold a consultation, after which they again drew near the white men, and at last a compromise was affected, the sorrowing relatives of the dead and wounded men receiving a blanket each, which was a good deal more than the rascals were worth, and the others some tobacco.

They now proceeded on their journey unmolested,

but the object of one party was utterly frustrated by the loss of the tin box, whose bearer soon recovered from the five gashes he had received in his head. They therefore all proceeded to the Oakanagan, on whose banks they found Mr. David Stuart and Mr. Ross well and flourishing, and after a stay of two or three days at the little station, they started for Astoria, accompanied by the former gentlemen.

On their journey down, after the forks of the Columbia had been passed, the inmates of the leading canoe were astonished to hear a voice from the bank hailing them in English, and on looking round, saw two miserable men entirely naked. In great wonder they paddled to the shore, and found these unhappy people to be Mr. Crooks and John Day, the Kentucky hunter.

I mentioned a few pages farther back that six of Mr. Hunt's party had not yet arrived at Astoria, having become so reduced by famine and exhaustion that the leader was compelled, for the preservation of the majority, to abandon them amongst the rocky defiles of the Snake River. This happened in December of the previous year, and the situation of these unfortunate people was rendered yet more precarious, owing to the main party having forcibly possessed themselves of the horses belonging to a band of Shoshone Indians, in whose vicinity the famished men were left, and whose vengeance they had just cause to dread. Most fortunately the Shoshones had never seen white men before, and therefore regarded them with a kind of superstitious fear; thus, although they speedily found out the retreat of the wanderers—for the illness of John Day caused Mr. Crooks to remain encamped at one spot for three weeks—they never attempted to molest them, though their tents were pitched close by, and finally the Indians withdrew altogether and were seen no more.

Day having recovered in some measure, the forlorn band crawled westward, subsisting on roots and crows, until the month of February, when three out of the four Canadians gave up the struggle for life, and refusing to go any further, were left—by their own wish—on the banks of a small stream, the three remaining men following Mr. Hunt's almost obliterated trail, and when that disappeared, wandering hopelessly in the mountains, living on such roots and berries as they could find, and occasionally killing a beaver, which was devoured to the very skin. At the end of March they fell in with another tribe of Shoshones, with whom the remaining Canadian decided to cast in his lot, but the more resolute Anglo-Saxons kept steadily on, and the snow diminishing in depth, they made a desperate and successful attempt to cross the last mountain range. Shortly after escaping from the barren wilderness that had for so long kept them prisoners, the two wanderers fell in with a tribe of Wallah-Wallah Indians, who received the starving men kindly, gave them plenty of horse-flesh to eat, and showed them the best route by which to reach the Columbia River. Aided by these instructions, they once more set forth, arrived at the mighty stream that flows past Astoria, and followed its course for over a hundred miles, when they were within a day's journey of the Cascades. Here they encountered some of the rascally pirates before mentioned, who pretended to receive them hospitably, but when their attention was diverted by the food the Indians set before them, these worthies seized their rifles, stripped them of the few rags that still clung to their emaciated limbs, and drove them forth into the wilderness unarmed and naked, refusing even to restore a flint and steel for which Mr. Crooks earnestly entreated them. Of the Cascade Indians an old trader says, "They are saucy, impudent rascals, who will steal when they can, and pillage whenever a weak party falls in their power." These words were penned long before the attack on Reed and the barbarity displayed towards Crooks and Day, and the writer must be felicitated on the just estimate of their character he then formed.

The two unhappy men were now in a more grievous state than ever, and resolved to return and throw themselves on the generosity of the hospitable Wallah-Wallahs, in pursuit of which determination they retraced their steps for eighty miles, and were on the point of leaving the Columbia and striking inland, when Stuart and his brigade of canoes appeared, and the wanderers were once more in safety amongst their friends, in company with whom they reached Astoria on the 11th of May, and found that the *Beaver*, a vessel despatched by Mr. Astor, had arrived at the settlement two days previously.

This ship brought considerable reinforcements to the colony, namely, another partner, five clerks, fifteen American labourers, and six Canadian *voyageurs*. Her captain, on leaving the Columbia, was to call at the Russian establishments at New Archangel, then to return to Astoria, and shipping all peltries, was to proceed direct to China, and there dispose of his valuable cargo. Elated by this addition to their numbers, and overjoyed at the knowledge that they were not altogether for-gotten by their friends, the Astorians set to work with renewed vigour. New expeditions were set afoot, two for the establishment of additional trading stations at the forks of the Columbia, where the rivalry of the North-West Company was feared ; one for Oakanagan, and a fourth for New York with despatches for Mr. Astor ; and the command of the latter, a work of great enterprise and danger, was entrusted to Mr. Robert Stuart, under whose command were placed four of the most experienced hunters in the settlement. McLellan determined on accompanying them, and to the surprise of everybody Mr. Crooks, undeterred by the fearful hardship he had just undergone, announced that he also should make one of the party.

As in the case of the former expeditions their road was the same for several hundred miles, and on the 29th of June the flotilla set forth in two barges and ten canoes, manned by about sixty hands, inclusive of the leaders. Before the first day had expired, John Day, the Kentucky hunter, and the companion of Mr. Crooks in his fearful journey, who was one of the men told off to accompany Stuart to the States, showed great agitation, and it became evident that privation and misery had affected his intellect. During their wanderings on the Snake River, Mr. Crooks had noticed symptoms of derangement, but hoping that a release from the horrors he had undergone would restore the balance of the noble fellow's mind, he had kept silence, but now concealment was useless, and as the canoes proceeded on their way, John Day became raving and incoherent. On seeing Indians his fury became unbounded, and mindful doubtless of their cruel conduct, he loaded them with abuse and maledictions. On the 2nd of July all doubt regarding his condition was removed by an attempt at suicide, but being disarmed, he professed great contrition and pretended to go to sleep, but in the early morning he sprang up suddenly, and seizing a brace of loaded pistols, attempted to blow out his brains. In his hurry he fired too high, and was immediately secured. To keep a constant watch over the poor fellow was impossible, and Mr. Stuart was much perplexed how to dispose of him ; however, some friendly Indians passed along, who promised to take him back to the settlement, and he was regretfully transferred to their canoe. They faithfully fulfilled their unenviable task, but the hunter's constitution and intellect were both worn out, and he gradually sank, until death, before the expiration of the year, released him from further suffering.

But the space at my command warns me that I must bring this brief sketch of Astoria to a close,

and return to the thread of my story and Paul
Gresham, whom I feel guilty of cruelly neglecting.
All the parties above described fulfilled their various
missions, Mr. Stuart's expedition reaching St. Louis
after a most painful journey, which occupied ten
months. But war had broken out between Great
Britain and the United States, and at any time
one of the British cruisers might cross the bar of
the Columbia River and commit Astoria to the
flames. The captain of the *Beaver* also, either
through ill-judgment or timidity, misconstrued his
orders, and a third ship sent forth by the indefatig-
able Mr. Astor was lost. In the face of so many
discouraging circumstances the further prosecution
of his gigantic scheme was abandoned by the great
American, and on the 16th of October, 1813, an
agreement was signed and executed, by which
all the peltry and merchandise of every kind
passed into the hands of the North-West Company, who made an uncommonly good bargain,
obtaining twenty thousand pounds' worth of furs
for about eight thousand pounds. Beaver was
valued at eight shillings per skin, though really
worth twenty; land otter at two shillings, though
worth fifteen; sea otter at three pounds, when
its proper price should have been from eight to
twelve.

So Astoria passed from the Americans to the British, and its name was changed to Fort George. I have, perhaps, entered rather at length into the history of this settlement, but it seemed to me that the record gives a clear insight into the dangers and privations of the fur trade, and is moreover too little known in Great Britain.

Perhaps the reader has not forgotten the tin box carried by Mr. Reed, and with one more anecdote regarding that luckless piece of tin I bid adieu to Astoria.

A very determined Scotchman named McKenzie was in charge of a canoe expedition, during the course of which he arrived at the portion of the Columbia on which was situated the village of Wish-ram, where lived the savages who had robbed and wounded Mr. Reed.   It was well known to the white men that both the "great medicine" box and rifle belonging to that gentleman were detained in the village as trophies, and, indignant at this, Mr. McKenzie offered to cross the river and demand the restoration of these articles if any one would accompany him.   Two volunteers at once presented themselves, and, despite the remonstrances of their companions, who knew what a hornet's nest they were about to enter, the trio shoved off in a canoe, and soon stepped ashore on the opposite bank.

Having looked carefully to the priming of their
rifles and pistols the three daring men followed
the path leading to the village, a narrow tortuous
way, winding about amongst rocks and boulders.
Their approach seemed quite unheeded by the
inhabitants ; no voice challenged the rash intruders ;
even the very dogs, usually so vociferous at the
approach of a stranger, were silent, and an unwonted stillness reigned around. With cautious
glances and light footsteps they pursued their way,
and in a few minutes stood within the pirate
stronghold ; and now a human being presented
itself, a young boy, who seemed aware of their
coming, and without breaking the ominious silence,
motioned the white men with his hand to enter a
house of much larger dimensions than its fellows,
standing in the centre of the village. Without
manifesting the slightest uneasiness, McKenzie
stooped his head and passed through the low door,
followed closely by his two companions. No
sooner were their feet over the threshold than from
some unseen quarter emerged a host of Indians,
whose dusky forms filled up the narrow passage,
and cut off all retreat.

But the three adventurers were men of unwavering determination, and, without betraying the
least hesitation, they coolly viewed the curious

scene before them. They were in a rudely built chamber of unusual size, measuring some twenty-five feet in length by twenty in breadth, at one end of which a large wood fire blazed, its fitful flame casting a flickering light on a semi-circle of grave, motionless red men, who, sitting three deep on the floor, wrapped in their buffalo robes, surrounded three sides of the apartment. One glance at the assemblage convinced the trio of the impossibility of retreat, and nothing remained but to carry out the rash adventure with hardihood. In the centre of the semi-circle, near the fire, sat the chief, an old warrior sixty years of age, who motioned them to take their seats on the vacant side of the room. In the midst of the same unbroken silence the white men complied, and an ominous pause ensued, during which the fierce eyes of the grim warriors flashed in the fire-light as they gazed scowlingly at their visitors. Well might the latter feel into what a scrape their recklessness had drawn them.

"Don't take your eye off the chief," whispered McKenzie, "I shall address him, and if you see him make the smallest sign to his band, shoot him through the heart, and make a rush for the door."

His companions nodded in acquiescence, and then McKenzie advanced towards the old chief, and offered him the pipe of peace. With an indignant wave of his arm the proffered token of amity was thrust aside, but, nothing daunted, the trader, who was thoroughly conversant with the Indian language, made a speech, in which he fearlessly acknowledged the object of their visit, and proposed to give a couple of blankets, an axe, some beads and tobacco, in exchange for the stolen rifle ; the " great medicine" box he said nothing about, for its contents were of little or no use to any one.

In unbroken silence the circle of motionless figures listened to the white man, and when he had finished, the chief, after an impressive pause, arose and commenced an harangue, low in tone at first, but becoming louder and louder as the orator worked himself up, until at last he shrieked out the words in the fury of his passion. He denounced the Astorians as mean and stingy, upbraiding them for their sordid conduct in using the river, and never making the slightest acknowledgment to the warriors dwelling on its banks, by whose sanction alone they could pass and repass, unless the latter had furs in their possession, when the white men were glad enough to trade. He stigmatised their conduct as paltry and low, and after raising the indignation of his warriors by recapitulating the circumstances attending the death of the man shot by McLellan, he concluded by threats of vengeance against all the settlers.

The three whites could see the eyes of their ferocious enemies blazing with suppressed wrath as their fancied grievances were laid before them by their chief, and it became evident that they were only awaiting his signal to rush upon their prey. But during the latter part of the speech McKenzie and his companions had risen to their feet, and had brought their rifles into position for immediate use; the muzzle of the leader's weapon being pointed full at the breast of the chief, and ready to send a bullet through his body at a distance little exceeding a yard, on the first suspicious movement. As the old warrior ceased speaking, McKenzie, keeping the weapon bearing full on him, cocked his rifle, and a crimson hue suffused the cheeks of the warriors as the click of the other two locks followed immediately afterwards.

" Follow me," cried McKenzie, and coolly but rapidly advanced towards the door, his rifle at full cock, and the barrel laying in the palm of his left hand ready for instant use.

"Give room," he cried to the throng outside prepared to oppose his exit, and, overawed at the bearing of the white men, the scowling savages fell back and suffered them to pass in safety. Taking the precaution to keep along the tops of the rocks, and by this means to avoid the devious path, in whose windings clusters of their enemies might yet be concealed, the adventurers reached their canoe in safety, and shortly afterwards their camp, having had about as narrow an escape of their lives as even they, in their adventurous career, could hope for.

CHAPTER XI.

WELL, Pierre, isn't it time Mr. Groves should turn up?" asked Paul, as he noticed his companion heaping fresh logs on the fire, and making sundry arrangements that manifested his intention to bestow himself beneath his buffalo robe, and become oblivious to the world around.

" *Oh, mais non, Monsieur Paul,* perhaps he find von Indian village, then he shall stay there till *demain.* Monsieur Groves he very good *chasseur,* suppose he no come by to-morrow night, then we go look. Now it time for the sleep. *Bon soir, monsieur,*" and without further parley the Canadian crept beneath his many coverings, and before five minutes had elapsed gave audible proof that he had wandered into sleep-land. Though his head was still running on the strange story that Lefranc had told him, our young friend was not long in following his example. At first he had some idea of remaining awake to welcome his friend Groves; but that gentleman's arrival seemed so problematical, that he dismissed it, and rolling himself up in his fur robes, was soon sound asleep.

By the time Paul and the Canadian had finished their breakfast on the following morning, Mr. Groves had not turned up; but seeing that his lengthened absence caused no alarm to Pierre, the young man said nothing beyond a casual remark, and with great alacrity slipping on his snow-shoes, followed the hunter to visit the traps they had made on the previous day. As on that occasion, the Canadian dragged after him the little hand-sleigh, which he hoped would be wanted to carry back the trapped game.

After about half an hour's walk, the moose skeleton, near which Pierre had set his wolf-gins, was reached, and here one trap was found missing, the trail in the snow plainly indicating in which direction the captured animal had dragged it. Within a hundred yards of the spot where it had been set, the stake at the end of the chain entangled in a bush, stood the gin, holding in its powerful jaws a handsome grey wolf, caught by the fore-leg. A blow on the head soon deprived it of life, and placing the carcase in the hand-sleigh, Pierre, having reset the gins, again moved forward. Paul was most anxious to see a marten caught, and

P

pressed onward eagerly when a trap was sighted, the Canadian following more leisurely with the sleigh. To the young man's great delight the "fall" was down, and sure enough under it lay a few scattered flecks of fur, but the animal from whence they came was absent.

"Some other animal must have eaten the marten after it was caught; a wolf, I dare say. No, that is never a wolf," he muttered, noticing a large footprint in the snow, "it must be a bear. Pierre," he shouted, "come along quickly. A bear has robbed the trap. Here are his tracks."

The Canadian hurried forward, and soon saw the state of the case.

"*Ce n'est pas un ours, c'est un carcajou, et tout est perdu,*" he said in a tone of extreme vexation. "We can go back to camp now, Monsieur Paul for the *carcajou* he rob every trap," and, irritated beyond measure, honest Pierre gave vent to some rather unparliamentary language in the various tongues of which he was master.

"What is a *carcajou*?" asked Paul, "I never heard the name before."

"*C'est un voleur*, a thief," replied the exasperated trapper; "you English call him the wolverene."

"Oh, a wolverene. But perhaps it is caught in one of the 'falls.'"

" Caught !" returned the Canadian in a tone of supreme disgust, "*vous le trouverez plus facile attraper le diable.* No, Monsieur Paul, when you know the *carcajou* better, you sall not talk of catching him in a trap. Come with me, and you shall see the mischiefs he do."

On arrival at the next "dead-fall" Paul saw with astonishment that the semi-circle of stones had been pulled down from the back, and the bait removed ; and at every single trap they visited, the same thing had occurred. Let us glance a little closer at the animal whose destructive propensities and cunning were now fully apparent to Paul.

The wolverene or glutton of naturalists (*Gulo Luscus*), and the *carcajou* of the Canadian *voya-geurs*, is a large animal with a head much resem-bling a dog's, being broad at the hinder part, much arched, and rounded on all sides. Its body is very long, stout, and compactly made, the back arched ; and the whole form clearly indicates immense strength without much agility. The legs are short and stout ; the feet broad, and clothed on the under surface with a compact mass of woolly hair, whilst the toes, which are armed with strong, rounded claws, cause the track left in the snow by this animal strongly to resemble that of the bear, so Paul in mistaking its footprint for that of the latter was not committing a great error in wood-craft. The tail of the wolverene is rather short, hangs low, and is covered with long pendulous hairs. In common with the other fur-bearing animals before described, it has two coats, an upper and an under. The latter is of a deep chestnut brown, a shade lighter near the roots ; whilst the longer hairs are blackish-brown throughout their whole length, and much resemble the fur of a bear. The eyes, nose, and whiskers are black ; a pale reddish-brown beard commences behind the shoulder and running along the flanks, turns up on the hip, and unites near the tail with similar markings on the opposite side. There is a brownish-white band across the forehead running from ear to ear. On the sides of the neck there are tufts of white hair extending nearly in a circle from the inside of the legs around the chest. The colour varies greatly in different specimens, hence many naturalists have attempted from these varieties to multiply the species, but the best authorities agree in regarding them as belonging to exactly the same. It was also once thought that the glutton and wolverene were distinct animals, but this is now recognised as an error.

The wolverene may be said to vie with the beaver in the numerous miraculous stories that have been

circulated and devoutly credited concerning its
cunning, ferocity, extreme wariness, and gorman-
dizing habits. Olaus Magnus, whose appetite for
the marvellous was insatiable, tells us, " It is wont,
when it has found the carcase of some large beast,
to eat until its belly is distended like a drum, when
it rids itself of its load by squeezing its body
betwixt two trees growing near together, and again
returning to its repast, soon requires to have re-
course to the same means of relief." Buffon,
following the reports of preceding writers, describes
it as a ferocious animal, which approaches man
without fear, and attacks the larger quadrupeds
without hesitation ; but he states that its pace is so
slow that it can take its prey only by surprise, to
accomplish which it employs an extraordinary
degree of cunning. To use his own words "the
defect of nimbleness he (the wolverene) supplies
with cunning ; he lies in wait for animals as they
pass, he climbs upon trees in order to dart upon
his prey and seize it with advantage ; he throws
himself down upon elks and reindeer, and fixes so
firmly on their bodies with his claws and teeth that
nothing can remove him. In vain do the poor
victims fly and rub themselves against trees ; the
enemy, attached to the crupper or neck, continues
to suck their blood, to enlarge the wound, and to

devour them gradually and with equal voracity, till they fall down.

"More insatiable and rapacious than the wolf, if endowed with equal agility, the glutton would destroy all the other animals; but he moves so heavily that the only animal he is able to overtake in the course is the beaver, whose cabins he sometimes attacks, and devours the whole unless they quickly take to the water, for the beaver outstrips him in swimming. When he perceives that his prey has escaped he seizes the fishes; and when he can find no living creature to destroy he goes in quest of the dead, whom he digs up from their graves, and devours with avidity." Buffon also terms the wolverene the "quadruped vulture," and repeats the old story that it entices reindeer to come beneath the tree within whose branches it lies concealed, by throwing down the moss which that animal is fond of; but all these stories are fictitious, and in a later edition of his work he corrects the errors of previous writers, and sweeps away most of the marvellous propensities attributed to the glutton, being the better enabled to do this from his personal observation, a friend having sent him a wolverene as a present, whose habits he carefully noted for eighteen months. In a supplementary chapter he informs us, "He was so tame that he discovered no ferocity, and did not injure any person. His voracity has been as much exaggerated as his cruelty; he indeed ate a great deal, but when deprived of food he was not importunate.

"The animal is pretty mild; he avoids water, and dreads horses and men dressed in black. He moves by a kind of leap, and eats pretty voraciously. After taking a full meal he covers himself in the cage with straw. When drinking he laps like a dog. He utters no cry. After drinking he throws the remainder of the water on his belly with his paws. He is almost perpetually in motion. If allowed, he would devour more than four pounds of flesh in a day; he eats no bread, and devours his food so voraciously, and almost without chewing, that he is apt to choke himself."

Before writing of this animal, I made a visit to the Zoological Gardens, for the express purpose of examining the specimen in the Society's possession. From all I could gather, the account given above by Buffon is correct, except as regards avoiding water, for during the half-hour or so I stood watching the animal he entered a large trough filled with water at least twenty times; neither did he manifest any dread of the black garments worn by my companion and myself. Messrs. Audubon and Bachman give the following account of an accidental meeting with a wolverene :—

"While hunting the northern hare, immediately after a heavy fall of snow, we unexpectedly came upon the track of an animal which at the time we supposed to be that of a bear, a species which even then was scarcely known in that portion of the country (which was already pretty thickly settled). We followed the broad trail over the hills and through the devious windings of the forest for about five miles, till within sight of a ledge of rocks on the banks of the Hoosack River, when, as we found the night approaching, we were reluctantly compelled to give up the pursuit for that day, intending to resume it on the following morning. It snowed incessantly for two days afterwards, and, believing that the bear had retired to his winter retreat, we concluded that the chance of adding it to our collection had passed by. Some weeks afterwards, a favourite servant, who was always anxious to aid us in our pursuits, and who not only knew many quadrupeds and birds, but was acquainted with many of their habits, informed us that he had on a previous day seen several tracks similar to those we had described, crossing a new road cut through the forest. As early on the following morning as we could see a track in the snow, we were fully accoutred, and with a gun and a pair of choice hounds, started on what we conceived our second bear hunt. Before reaching the spot where the tracks had been observed, however, we met a fresh trail of the previous night, and pursued it without loss of time. The animal had joined some foxes which were feeding on a dead horse not a hundred yards from a log cabin in the forest, and after having satiated itself with this delicate food, made directly for the Hoosack River, pursuing the same course along which we had formerly traced it. To our surprise it did not cross the river, now firmly bound with ice, but retired to its burrow, which was not far from the place where we had a few weeks before abandoned the pursuit of it. The hounds had not once broke into full cry upon the track, but no sooner had they arrived at the mouth of the burrow than they rushed into the large opening between the rocks, and commenced a furious attack on the animal within. This lasted but for a few moments, and they came out as quickly as they had entered. They showed some evidence of having been exposed to sharp claws and teeth, and although they had been only a moment engaged in battle, had no disposition to renew it. No effort of ours could induce them to re-enter the cavern, whilst their furious barking at the mouth of the hole was answered by a grow. from within. The animal, although not ten feet from the entrance, could not be easily reached with a stick, on account of his having retreated behind an angle in the chasm. As we felt no particular disposition to imitate the exploits of Colonel Putnam in his encounter with the wolf, we reluctantly concluded to trudge homeward through the snow, a distance of five miles, to obtain assistance. On taking another survey of the place, however, we conceived it possible to effect an opening on one of its sides. This was after great labour accomplished by prying away some heavy fragments of the rock. The animal could now be reached with a pole, and seemed very much irritated, growling and snapping at the stick, which he once succeeded in tearing from our hand, all the while emitting a strong and very offensive musky smell. He was finally shot. What was our surprise and pleasure on discovering that we had, not a bear, but what was more valuable to us, a new species of quadruped, as we believed it to be. It was six months before we were enabled, by consulting a copy of Buffon, to discover our mistake, and ascertain that our highly-prized specimen was the glutton, of which we had read such marvellous tales in the school-books."

All travellers in the Hudson's Bay Territory, from Ellis and Pennant in early days, to Lord Milton and Dr. Cheadle in our own time, unite in testifying to the wonderful perseverance of the wolverene in following the footsteps of the trappers in order to obtain the bait, or to devour the animals that may have been caught therein. In an old book now before me, Hearn's Journey to the Northern Ocean, a curious record of the perseverance and pluck of a Hudson's Bay officer, I find many anecdotes of the various animals encountered by the traveller in his wanderings; and amongst others the following account of the wolverene, which I venture to extract at length, as the original work is scarce, and not likely to fall into the hands of the majority of readers.

"The wolverene is common in the Northern regions as far north as the Copper River, and perhaps farther. They are equally the inhabitants of woods and barren grounds; for the Esquimaux to the north of Churchill kill many of them when their skins are in excellent season: a proof of their being capable of bearing the severest cold. They are very slow in their pace, but their wonderful sagacity, strength, and acute scent, make ample amends for that defect; for they are seldom killed at any season when they do not prove very fat:

a great proof of their being excellent providers. With respect to the fierceness of this animal which some assert, I can say little, but I know them to be beasts of great courage and resolution, for I once saw one of them take possession of a deer that an Indian had killed, and though the Indian advanced within twenty yards, he would not relinquish his claim to it, but suffered himself to be shot standing on the deer.   I once saw a similar instance of a lynx, or wild cat, which also suffered itself to be killed before it would relinquish the prize.   The wolverenes have also frequently been seen to take a deer from a wolf before the latter had time to begin his repast after killing it.   Indeed their amazing strength, and the length and sharpness of their claws, render them capable of making a strong resistance against any other animal in those parts, the bear not excepted.   As a proof of their amazing strength, there was one at Churchill some years since, that overset the greatest part of a large pile of wood (containing a whole winter's firing, that measured upwards of seventy yards round), to get at some provisions that had been hid there by the Company's servants, when going to the factory to spend the Christmas holidays.   The fact was, this animal had been lurking about in the neighbour-hood of their tent (which was about eight miles

from the factory) for some weeks, and had committed many depredations on the game caught in
their traps and snares, as well as eaten many foxes
that were killed by guns set for that purpose ; but
the wolverene was too cunning to take either trap
or gun himself. The people knowing the mischievous disposition of those animals, took (as they
thought) the most effectual method to secure the
remains of their provisions, which they did not
choose to carry home, and accordingly tied it up in
bundles and placed it on the top of the wood-pile
(about two miles from their tent), little thinking
the wolverene would find it out ; but to their great
surprise, when they returned to their tent after the
holidays, they found the pile of wood in the state
already mentioned, though some of the trees that
composed it were as much as two men could carry.
The only reason the people could give for the
animal doing so much mischief was, that in his
attempting to carry off the booty, some of the
small parcels of provisions had fallen down into
the heart of the pile, and sooner than lose half his
prize, he pursued the above method till he had
accomplished his ends. The bags of flour, oatmeal,
and pease, though of no use to him, he tore all to
pieces, and scattered the contents about on the
snow ; but every bit of animal food, consisting of

beef, pork, bacon, venison, salt geese, partridges, &c., to a considerable amount, he carried away. These animals are great enemies to the beaver, but the manner of life of the latter prevents them from falling into their clutches so frequently as many other animals; they commit vast depredations on the foxes during the summer, while the young ones are small; their quick scent directs them to their dens, and if the entrance be too small, their strength enables them to widen it, and go in and kill the mother and all her cubs. In fact, they are the most destructive animals in this country."

Other travellers and naturalists are equally ready to chronicle the misdeeds of the wolverene. Sir John Richardson, in his Fauna Boreali-Americana, says: "It is a carnivorous animal, which feeds chiefly upon the carcases of beasts that have been killed by accident. It has great strength, and annoys the natives by destroying their hoards of provision, and demolishing their marten traps. It is so suspicious, that it will rarely enter a trap itself, but beginning behind, pulls it to pieces, scatters the logs of which it is built, and then carries off the bait. It feeds also on meadow mice, marmots, and other *rodentia*, and occasionally on disabled quadrupeds of a larger size. I have seen one chasing an American hare, which was at the

same time harassed by a snowy owl. It resembles
the bear in its gait, and is not fleet ; but it is very
industrious, and no doubt feeds well, as it is
generally fat. It is much abroad in the winter, and
the track of its journey in a single night might be
often traced for many miles. From the shortness
of its legs, it makes its way through loose snow
with difficulty, but when it falls upon the beaten
track of a marten trapper it will pursue it for a long
way." Mr. Graham observes that " the wolverenes
are extremely mischievous, and do more damage to
the small fur trade than all the other rapacious
animals conjointly. They will follow the marten
hunters' path round a line of traps extending forty,
fifty, or sixty miles, and render the whole un-
serviceable, merely to come at the baits, which are
generally the head of a partridge or a bit of dried
venison. They are not fond of the martens themselves, but never fail of tearing them in pieces or of
burying them in the snow by the side of the path,
at a considerable distance from the trap. Drifts of
snow often conceal the repositories thus made of the
martens from the hunter, in which case they furnish
a regale to the hungry fox, whose sagacious nostril
guides him unerringly to the spot. Two or three
foxes are often seen following the wolverene for
this purpose."

One more quotation, and I have finished. Captain Cartwright says : " In coming to the foot of Table Hill I crossed the track of a wolverene with one of Mr. Callingham's traps on his foot ; the foxes had followed his bleeding track. As this beast went through the thick of the woods, under the north side of the hill, where the snow was so deep and light that it was with the greatest difficulty I could follow him, even in Indian rackets, I was quite puzzled to know how he had contrived to prevent the trap from catching hold of the branches of the trees or sinking in the snow. But on coming up with him I discovered how he had managed ; for after making an attempt to fly at me, he took the trap in his mouth and ran upon three legs. These creatures are surprisingly strong in proportion to their size ; this weighed only twenty-six pounds and the trap eight, yet, including all the turns he had taken, he had carried it six miles."

The usual length of the wolverene is from two feet six to two feet ten inches, exclusive of the tail ; and now I think I have occupied as much space as I dare with the curious animal whom, with the beaver, I have selected to give a name to this little volume.

" Well, Pierre," said Paul, " what is to be done now ; shall we set the traps afresh ? "

" *C'est inutile, Monsieur Paul,* we must try to catch two or three beaver, and then we shall move away. I only hope the rascal *carcajou* he no follow us;" and with a sigh at so much labour misspent, the Canadian led the way towards a small frozen stream, where he knew the beavers had a settlement.

CHAPTER XII.

N hour's walk on their snow-shoes brought the trappers to a little lake, frozen firmly over, and covered with a sheet of purest snow. At the spot where the small stream mentioned in the last chapter fell into the lake, Paul observed many oven-shaped excrescences; these, his companion informed him, were the lodges of the beavers, and within them the animals lay comfortably asleep. Under Pierre's direction several small saplings were felled, and by sharpening their ends were fashioned into stout stakes. All was now in readiness, and the Canadian carefully examined the ground and the frozen surface of the lake, to ascertain at what points the beavers communicated with their retreats in the bank. A skilled trapper, he was not long in finding out these weak places; and cutting away the ice he drove stakes into the passage, so that both entry and exit were effectually cut off. Proceeding to the lodges, a similar method was adopted, the thick ice removed with axe and chisel, and the stakes driven in close to the apertures by which the animals communicated with their holes in the bank. Thus it will be seen that the beavers were fairly pent in wherever they might be : if they were in the bank, stout stakes prevented their return to the lodges ; and if in the latter, similar obstacles cut off their escape to the shore.

"Now, *Monsieur Paul*, we shall have *beaucoup de travaille*, plenty of work to keep us warm ;" and thus saying, the Canadian seized his ice chisel—an iron instrument resembling, but stouter than an ordinary chisel, fitted to a long wooden handle— and commenced a vigorous attack upon the summit of the nearest lodge. It is perhaps difficult to imagine that a powerful man, expert in the use of his tools, should find it hard work to break through the wood and plaster fabric erected by a few little animals no bigger than an ordinary terrier, but after half an hour of chipping and digging Pierre was glad to relinquish the chisel for a few minutes to his companion, the perspiration standing on his brow in beads, which in a few seconds became little studs of ice. An hour and a half elapsed before the interior of the lodge was laid open, for it was over six feet in thickness and frozen as solid as granite; but at last the interior was reached, and the poor sleepy beavers dragged ruthlessly from their winter retreat, killed by a blow on the nose, and deposited in the hand-sleigh. So the hunters proceeded until a dozen animals had fallen victims, when the approach of dusk warned them to desist, and they proceeded to camp with their game.

Pierre was in advance dragging the little sleigh, and when within a quarter of a mile of the camp, Paul remarked that he came to a standstill and examined the snow carefully.

"What is the matter, Pierre?" asked the young man.

The Canadian pointed to the track of a pair of snow-shoes, not going straight to or from the camp, but seemingly following a circular direction, as though the wearer had wished to examine the locality without approaching too closely.

"It must be Groves, Pierre, let us hurry on and join him."

"*Ce n'est pas Monsieur Groves*, it is an Indian."

"How can you tell that?"

"You look at the track, *Monsieur Paul*. Your friend he very good *chasseur*, but he no make a trail *comme ça*. That one Indian, who been walk all his life on snow-shoes."

" Paul looked attentively, and saw that the hunter was right. The footprints were even in depth and equidistant, whilst the furrow left by dragging the shoes forward was straight and clearly defined. Evidently the stranger was thoroughly habituated to this mode of travelling.

"Well, Pierre, if it is an Indian, what does it matter? He won't attempt to harm us, will he?"

"*Non, monsieur*, but some Indians just as bad as the rascal *cacajou*. Perhaps he steal our blankets and traps."

This was a new idea to Paul, who shivered beneath his fur clothing at the thought of passing a night exposed to the full severity of such weather.

"*En avant, monsieur*," cried the Canadian, "we shall soon find out;" and seizing the cord attached to the hand-sleigh, he set off camp-ward with such speed that Paul, less experienced, was fairly distanced.

Pierre's joyous shout soon reached him, and on arriving he found his companion already busy at replenishing the fire, and getting ready for supper. Everything was exactly as they had left it in the morning, and no strange foot-prints in the snow indicated that the stranger had even seen the encampment.

The evening meal was finished, the pipes lit, and the two occupants of the camp had bestowed themselves in lounging attitudes beside the ample fire. Neither talked much, for Paul was admiring the silent beauty of the snow-sheeted lake, over whose crisp and smooth expanse the moon was sailing in silver splendour, and the Canadian was probably engaged in determining whose were the foot-prints that he felt conscious had made a circuit of the camp. After some ten minutes of silence the latter arose, and lifting a huge log in his brawny arms flung it on to the fire, sending a thousand ruddy sparks upward to the branches of the old pine. The flames leapt greedily to devour the new comer, the sudden crackle of the dry bark forming a strange contrast to the dead silence reigning without. As the trapper stretched forth his hands to meet the welcome warmth and drew his lofty figure up to its full height, Paul perceived a form rise from behind the bushes that bordered the margin of the lake, but e'er he had time to call his companion's attention, the sharp crack of a rifle rang ominously through the air, and with a sudden exclamation the Canadian staggered backward and fell amongst the snow, whose pure surface was soon stained with a crimson hue. To dart forward to his wounded companion was, for Paul, but the work of a moment, and exerting all his strength, he managed to lift the huge form of the *voyageur* and deposit it on the buffalo robes, and as he did so his eye caught the outline of a human figure as it glided silently away into the depths of the forest.

"By heaven, there is the murderer escaping," he cried, snatching up his rifle.

"*Suivez-le, Monsieur Paul*," said Lefranc, eagerly.

"But how can I leave you, my poor fellow?" replied the young man.

"*Je suis seulement blessé*, it is nothing; follow and see the direction he take, you can come back soon."

The whole of the above scene occupied only a few seconds, and without a moment's hesitation or reflection Paul slipped on his snow-shoes, and rifle in hand darted off in pursuit of the flying figure, now barely visible amongst the forest trees. The fugitive was following a course that would lead him near the skeleton of the moose, but great was Paul's mortification to find that at every pace he lost ground; even in the uncertain moonlight he could not but perceive that his enemy was increasing the distance between them at every step. Still he struggled on manfully, indignant at the base attempt on the Canadian's life, and hoping that some unforeseen accident would enable him to overtake the assassin; but like a sombre ghost amidst the whiteness of the landscape, the dark figure threaded its way through the intricacies of the forest, and the young man felt at length that to continue the chase would be useless.

"At all events, I have driven the scoundrel a good long way from the camp," he muttered ; "and now to return and look after poor Pierre. By Jove, what can that be," he added, as the rattle of iron met his ear, coming from the direction in which the murderer had vanished.

All thought of retreat was cast aside now, and Paul dashed forward at headlong speed, casting up the drift snow in clouds from the rapid movements of his snow-shoes. At every stride the rattle of the chain became more audible, and as the young man reached the edge of a little open glade on which the moon shed its welcome light, the reason of the noise became apparent. There stood the dark figure he had chased in vain, but all its airiness of motion had departed, for in his hurried flight the murderer had traversed the spot where his victim had planted the wolf-traps, one of which was firmly attached to his leg, whilst the powerful spring of the other had broken the tough framework of his snow-shoe.

As Paul emerged from the forest, the assassin succeeded in freeing his leg, but on a single snow-shoe escape was hopeless ; so, slipping his foot out of the remaining one, he stood upon his guard, and a bullet whistling through Paul's floating locks warned him that the wasp had yet power to sting. But dauntlessly the young man held upon his course, his rifle at full cock, and its muzzle directed towards the breast of his enemy, whom he now perceived to be an Indian of gigantic stature.

"*Rendez-vous*," he shouted, "*ou je tire!;*" but the grim warrior disdained to yield, and Paul steadily advanced, determined not to fire until so close that missing his aim would be impossible.

With his eye fixed upon every movement of the Indian, Paul lessened the distance between them, and now but half a dozen paces separated him from his adversary.

"One yard nearer and I will fire, unless he surrenders," thought the young man, as he stepped forward ; but, his gaze fixed steadily on the foe, he had not noticed, lying half buried in the snow, the steel trap from which the Indian had just escaped. In the closed semi-circular jaws of this his snow-shoe became entangled, and for one brief instant his gaze was removed from his antagonist and directed to the ground in search of the impediment. That fleeting moment sufficed for the watchful red man ; with one bound he cleared the distance that separated him from Paul, and locked in each other's arms a death struggle commenced.

And now, Paul Gresham, it were best to call to remembrance every trick of wrestling that the gymnasium taught, or you will hardly escape from the sinewy arms that are pressing you to the dusky breast with a grip like that of an angry bear. Under the vice-like pressure the very ribs of the young man seem to yield, and a lengthened resistance is plainly impossible. But does the Indian know the Cornish back-throw with which Johnny Treglowin vanquished the town bully in an Oxford row, and which Johnny had taught Paul? No. With an adroit movement the Englishman obtained a shift of position, and another moment saw the Indian pitched head foremost into the trampled snow.

To stoop for the rifle, which had been knocked from his grasp at the commencement of the struggle, was the young man's first impulse; and, luckily, a moonbeam glinting on the barrel revealed its whereabouts. Now he thought himself safe, and his fingers wandered to the lock, with whose touch he was so familiar; it was strange, he had picked up the Indian's empty musket.

But there was no time to rectify the error, and Paul was just able to club the weapon before his antagonist sprang forward to renew the attack. In desperation he swept the gun round with the full strength of both arms, and the Indian, confused probably by his heavy fall, strove in vain to avoid the blow ; the flint lock struck the murderer under the ear, and his huge form toppled helplessly to the earth.

Paul stood bewildered for some moments, and then bent over his recent antagonist, whose heavy breathing announced that life was not extinct. By the merest accident the young man had left the camp with a flask in his pocket, so kneeling down beside the prostrate warrior, he raised his head, and poured a few spoonfuls of undiluted rum down his throat.

" Surely I have seen that fellow before," thought Paul, as the moonbeams lighted on the Indian's face. " Yes, now I remember, it is *Tête-de-bois*, the Ojibbeway with whom poor Pierre had the quarrel, and of whom the ' Violet' always warned her husband to beware. Well, he must remain there for the present at all events, and I must hurry back to the Canadian."

As Paul drew near the encampment he was astonished to see several forms moving round the fire, and to hear the jingle of sleigh-bells as the horses shook their heads ; but his wonder was increased to amazement when a figure advanced to meet him, and a familiar voice cried out " Well. dear old Paul, how delighted I am to see you."

" Why, George Marshall, what, in the name of fortune, brings *you* here ?

" Only to tell you good news, old fellow, and to see the country a little for myself."

" But how did you know we were camped here?"

" Oh! Mr. Groves brought us. We met him at an Ojibbeway village, where he had strayed in following up some moose."

" And how is poor Pierre ?"

" He will do well enough," said Groves, who had joined; " it is only a flesh wound, and the 'Violet' will soon put that to rights. We have sent him off to Osnaburg House in the sleigh, which will return for us to-morrow."

" Then let us bring in the Indian that I knocked down, or he will perish from exposure."

The young men hastened to the scene of the struggle, but *Tête-de-bois* had disappeared.

" Here are his tracks," cried Paul, pointing to the trodden snow, "the rascal has come to his senses and crept away."

" And by far the best thing that could happen," said Groves. " We should only have been bothered to know how to deal with him. Let us hasten back to the fire, for these night rambles are not pleasant, with the thermometer below zero."

There was much conversation over the camp

fire that night. Groves related how he had followed up the moose steadily, and had succeeded in killing the old cow and both her calves. Some Ojibbeway Indians who were hunting in the neighbourhood had joined him, and their chief, *Tête-de-bois*, had induced him to return to their village, undertaking to look after the transport of the venison himself. This was after the chief had heard that Pierre Lefranc was encamped on the lake with only Paul as a companion, and was a strategem to enable *Tête-de-bois* to revenge himself on the Canadian, against whom he had long borne a deadly hatred. During the short time that Groves was at the Indian village, George Marshall arrived with three or four sleighs ; for, being the son and heir of a powerful director, he travelled with even more pomp than Mr. Tanner.

George explained the cause of his unexpected arrival.

"You know," he said, "how much I wished my father to let me accompany you at first, and you know how persistently he refused. Well, when news arrived that the American House whose failure had caused Mr. Gresham's death was about to pay eighteen shillings in the pound, he could not deny my request to be the bearer of the news that you are, if not a millionaire, at all events a rich man. I started off immediately from Liverpool, and thanks to the courtesy of Mr. Tanner, here I am. I propose looking about me a little and then taking a trip on the prairies, in which I thought you would accompany me ; for as we are both out in America, there is no good in returning until we have seen all the lions."

"Ah, you are lucky fellows," sighed poor Groves.

"Well, of course I am glad to hear that my worldly position is better, and you are a good fellow for coming so far to see me," said Paul, affectionately squeezing his old friend's hand ; "but let us go to sleep now, or we shall be fit for nothing in the morning. Pah! how that warrior's eyes seem to glare in my face."

The young men stretched themselves beneath their buffalo robes, and silence reigned throughout the encampment, though I much question whether sleep visited any of their eyes. And in the stillness of that snow-clad Canadian wilderness I shall take leave of them for the present, though perhaps on some future day their further adventures, amongst the buffaloes and grizzly bears of the Far West, will be presented to the reader.

THE END.

LONDON:
PRINTED BY JAS. TRUSCOTT AND SON,
Suffolk Lane, City.

PUBLICATIONS

OF THE

Society for Promoting Christian Knowledge.

Most of these Works may be had in Ornamental Bindings,
with Gilt Edges, at a small extra charge.

s. d.

MATE OF THE "LILY" (THE); OR, NOTES FROM HARRY MUSGRAVE'S LOG-BOOK. By the late WILLIAM H. G. KINGSTON, author of "Owen Hartley," &c. With Three full-page Illustrations on toned paper. Crown 8vo. .... *Cloth boards* 1 6

MRS. DOBBS' DULL BOY. By ANNETTE LYSTER, author of "Northwind and Sunshine," &c. With Three full-page Illustrations on toned paper. Crown 8vo. .... *Cloth boards* 2 6

NOT A SUCCESS. By the author of "Our Valley," "The Children of Sceligsberg," &c. With Three full-page Illustrations on toned paper. Crown 8vo. .... *Cloth boards* 1 6

PERCY TREVOR'S TRAINING. By the author of "Two Voyages," &c. With Three full-page Illustrations on toned paper. Crown 8vo. .... *Cloth boards* 2 6

PHILIP VANDELEUR'S VICTORY. By C. H. EDEN, author of "Australia's Heroes," "The Fifth Continent," &c. With Three full-page Illustrations on toned paper. Crown 8vo. *Cloth boards* 2 6

RECLAIMED. A Tale. By the Rev. A. EUBULE-EVANS. With Three Illustrations on toned paper. Crown 8vo. *Cloth boards* 2 6

ROUND MY TABLE. By H. L. C. P., author of "The Topmost Bough," &c. With Three full-page Illustrations on toned paper. Crown 8vo. ....*Cloth boards* 1 6

SNOW FORT AND THE FROZEN LAKE (THE); OR, CHRISTMAS HOLIDAYS AT POND HOUSE. By EADGYTH. With Three full-page Illustrations on toned paper. Crown 8vo. *Cloth boards* 2 6

STEFFAN'S ANGEL, AND OTHER STORIES. By M. E. TOWNSEND. With Three page Illustrations on toned paper. Crown 8vo. ....*Cloth boards* 2 6

STORIES FROM ITALIAN HISTORY. By B. MONTGOMERIE RANKING. With Two full-page Illustrations on toned paper. Crown 8vo...*Cloth boards* 1 6

THROUGH THE ROUGH WIND. A Story of the Collieries. By CRONA TEMPLE, author of "Etta's Fairies," &c. With Three full-page Illustrations on toned paper. Crown 8vo. *Cloth boards* 1 6

TWO SHIPMATES (THE). By the late W. H. G. KINGSTON, author of "Ned Garth," &c., &c. With Three full-page Illustrations on toned paper. Crown 8vo. ....*Cloth boards* 1 6

LONDON:

SOCIETY FOR PROMOTING CHRISTIAN KNOWLEDGE,

NORTHUMBERLAND AVENUE, CHARING CROSS, W.C. ;

43, QUEEN VICTORIA STREET, E.C.

BRIGHTON: 135, NORTH STREET.